Angel Teachers

Other Titles by William L. Fibkins

An Administrator's Guide to Better Teacher Mentoring, Second Edition

*Stopping the Brain Drain of Skilled Veteran Teachers:
Retaining and Valuing their Hard-Won Experience*

Teen Obesity: How Schools Can Be the Number One Solution to the Problem

Innocence Denied: A Guide to Preventing Sexual Misconduct by Teachers and Coaches

Students in Trouble Schools Can Help Before Failure

An Educator's Guide to Understanding the Personal Side of Students' Lives

An Administrator's Guide to Better Teacher Mentoring

Angel Teachers

Educators Who Care about Troubled Teens

William L. Fibkins

ROWMAN & LITTLEFIELD EDUCATION
A division of
ROWMAN & LITTLEFIELD PUBLISHERS, INC.
Lanham • New York • Toronto • Plymouth, UK

Published by Rowman & Littlefield Education
A division of Rowman & Littlefield Publishers, Inc.
A wholly owned subsidiary of The Rowman & Littlefield Publishing Group, Inc.
4501 Forbes Boulevard, Suite 200, Lanham, Maryland 20706
www.rowman.com

10 Thornbury Road, Plymouth PL6 7PP, United Kingdom

Copyright © 2012 by William L. Fibkins

All rights reserved. No part of this book may be reproduced in any form or by any electronic or mechanical means, including information storage and retrieval systems, without written permission from the publisher, except by a reviewer who may quote passages in a review.

British Library Cataloguing in Publication Information Available

Library of Congress Cataloging-in-Publication Data
Fibkins, William L.
Angel teachers : educators who care about troubled teens / William L. Fibkins.
p. cm.
Includes bibliographical references.
ISBN 978-1-61048-594-4 (pbk. : alk. paper)—ISBN 978-1-61048-595-1 (electronic)
1. Teacher participation in educational counseling. 2. Counseling in secondary education. 3. Teacher-student relationships. I. Title.
LB1027.5.F49 2012
371.4'046—dc23
2012024413

Contents

Introduction   vii

1   There Are Angel Teachers in Many Secondary Schools. We Need More.   1

2   The Kinds of Problems Troubled Teens Bring to Angel Teachers   27

3   The Presence of Angel Teachers Might Save the Lives of Desperate Teenagers   61

4   The Skills, Concerns, Issues, and Ongoing Training Needs of Angel Teachers   71

5   How to Upgrade the Skills of Angel Teachers and Get More Subject Matter Teachers on Board   79

References   99

About the Author   101

Introduction

We know teenagers face many developmental issues as they navigate their paths into adult life. They sometimes find themselves heading towards the margins of school life because of academic failure, poor peer relations, acting-out behaviors, and school and home pressures. These problems often lead to risky behaviors with drugs, alcohol, and tobacco that in the end only complicate their young lives and offer them little relief. They need help, support, and guidance from caring and experienced adults who can help them redirect their lives.

However, "help," as it is organized in our large high schools, junior high schools, and middle schools, is usually centered on a few overworked guidance counselors, social workers, and school psychologists who increasingly find themselves losing staff due to budget cuts. As a result school communities find themselves in a no-win situation in which the needs and problems of teenagers are on the rise while the core of designated helpers in the school organization is being decimated. They are forced to abandon their helping and counseling roles in order to take on administrative duties because of cuts in administrative staff. This we know. It is the new reality in our secondary schools.

There is a glimmer of hope in this dire scenario. It has given rise to the need for caring and experienced teachers to be given the green light to open their doors to kids in need. As any wise educator knows, this is not a new role for teachers who see their role as not only academic teachers but as personal advisors as well. They are what I call "angel teachers." They are educators who truly care about kids' well-being.

We can find these teachers in most secondary schools. They carry on their interventions with students in a quiet, trusting, private manner with little interest in notoriety or stardom. In fact, that's why kids in need are attracted to them and line up outside their doors. Kids know these caring teachers can deliver the kinds of help they need. They are savvy and know the drill of how help works for kids in need.

But the valuable, helping work of these angel teachers has often gone unheralded because the designated helpers in the school have been anointed with that role. Today's circumstances call for change if our schools are to meet the personal and well-being needs of their students. We need to examine the role of these teachers and make the case that they are now needed to take a primary role in the schools' intervention efforts.

This is a story of educators who are skilled and motivated and who, while not fearless, make a conscious effort to help teens whom they see at risk, heading towards failure and the margins of school life. Keep in mind that teens in need of intervention and support come from all segments of the school population. They are not just teens who are acting out and failing but also highly motivated and successful teens, the standard bearers who tire of the pressure of being high achievers and are looking for a way out of the pressurized world no one wants them to abandon because they represent an example of how the school district is succeeding at academic excellence.

What is special and unique about these angel teachers who don't turn the other way when they see teens in trouble? How do they arrive at this commitment, what sustains them when they are initially rejected by troubled teens, and what sustains them when colleagues and the school's designated helpers critically question why they seem to have what it takes to deliver help? Sometimes it takes only one educator to help when all seems lost.

This book will explain how angel teachers choose helping roles in addition to their roles as academic teachers, by answering the following questions:

1. Why do some teachers choose to take on the role of angel teacher?
2. What are their skills?

3. Are some angel teachers "natural" helpers or is their craft honed over time with hard-earned experiences? Or both? Are their natural gifts supported by dedication, commitment, and ongoing learning, training, and mentoring?
4. What are some examples of how angel teachers forge helping relationships with troubled teens?
5. What are the hazards and risks in the role of angel teacher? For example, why do some counselors, school social workers, school psychologists, colleagues, administrators, parents, community members, and outside counseling professionals oppose this role?
6. How do angel teachers avoid becoming enamored of their special place in the school helping hierarchy?
7. How do angel teachers avoid becoming messiah teachers and becoming too involved with needy students?
8. How do the school leaders expand the corps of angel teachers so that quality intervention is easily accessible for students to help solve their growing academic, personal, and well-being needs?

The words of education reformer Bill Gates remind us of the great need for more angel teachers by suggesting, "America's high schools are obsolete. They were designed fifty years ago to meet the needs of another age. Until we design them to meet the needs of the 21st century, we will keep limiting, even ruining, the lives of millions of Americans every year. . . . But these are our high schools that keep letting kids drop through the cracks, and we act as if it can't be helped. We designed the schools, we can redesign them. The basic building of better high schools includes making sure kids have a number of adults who know them, look out for them, and push them to succeed."[1]

NOTE

1. Bill and Melinda Gates Foundation, "National Education Summit on High Schools," February 26, 2005, 1–5, blogoehlert.typepad.com/eclippings/2005/05/bill_gates_amer.html, accessed October 25, 2011.

Chapter One

There Are Angel Teachers in Many Secondary Schools. We Need More.

Teachers who care about students, are motivated, and have the skills to help them are necessary if we expect kids to grow up to be caring and productive citizens. The actor Martin Sheen, starring in the Broadway play "The Subject Was Roses," a portrait of a family in shambles, advises us that "we're all struggling with the basic need to know our worth; love is so scarce and this play focuses on that. If you don't leave home with the true sanctity of being, you won't see that sanctity in anyone else."[1]

That statement is true not only for kids in need but also for teachers whose work, if successful, requires them to see sanctity in all their students. Closing the emotional distance between teachers and their students, and between teachers and their colleagues, can help members of the school community see the goodness, the positives, in each other, not just the dark sides.

Each of them can come to believe that they are part of a school community in which they are known well and cared for. They can come to believe that, when trouble visits them, they have the will, skills, and support, as the playwright Horton Foote says, "to go on." Foote writes, "I don't know how people carry on. I've known people that the world has thrown everything at to discourage them, kill them, to break their spirit. And yet something about them retains a dignity. They face life and they don't ask quarters."[2]

That's the kind of students we want to develop—resilient, tough, knowing how to develop support from someone in their corner to help when needed, and knowing they have the responsibility and helping skills to do the same for others in need. The angel teachers I've known, worked side by side with, and admired understand this educative process and believe that a major part of their role is to model and teach kids how to go on and face life when others try to discourage them and break their spirit.

As educators we know that teenagers face many developmental issues as they navigate the path to adult life. They sometimes find themselves heading towards the margins of school life because of myriad problems—school failure, poor peer relations, academic pressure to succeed, acting-out behaviors, or family disturbances. These problems can lead to risky choices when seeking relief, often in drug, alcohol, or tobacco addictions. Such solutions in the beginning quiet their demons but over time further complicate their young lives and offer little relief, only more pain and increased isolation.

These kinds of problems can visit any member of the student community, not just the so-called at-risk teens—the high-achieving students who are the school's standard bearers; the star athletes; the average students who are seen as well-behaved, good kids who offer no trouble; the acting-out students who create mischief; failing students on the road to dropping out; or students addicted to drugs, alcohol, and tobacco. No one is immune to risks and taking a harmful path when the bottom falls out of their lives. Some have problems of their own making but more often problems caused by circumstances beyond their control.

These kids need help, support, and guidance from caring and experienced educators to help them redirect their lives before their problems become unmanageable and out of control. Often teachers who have a reputation of helping teens in trouble are very visible in school hallways, the cafeteria, and in extracurricular activities. They know how to deliver help in a quiet, trustworthy, and supportive manner and they know how to refer teens who may need more intensive help. They are angel teachers.

They are a guiding spirit and influence on troubled students. They know their students well, look out for them, and encourage them to come to school and be achievers even when their personal and academic lives are in disarray. Sadly though, there aren't enough angel teachers in our schools who are able to intervene and help troubled teens. We need more of them.

Angel teachers can be found in almost every high school, junior high, and middle school. When observing student-teacher interaction in these schools, one often hears a student advising a peer, "Go see Mr. Toomey or Ms. Tracy, they know how to help kids with problems. You can trust them. They know the deal, believe me. Let me take you up to Toomey's room after school. He's my academic advisor. You'll feel better after talking to him."

Students are savvy about who delivers help and who doesn't in their schools. As the saying goes, they "know the drill." Although the school's public relations information suggests that guidance counselors, social workers, and school psychologists are the designated helpers for student troubles, students know that the counselor's role in helping has been limited by having too many administrative duties, such as scheduling classes for students, administering the increased number of mandated tests, and the ever-increasing demands of guiding students into the "right" colleges.

Students understand that budget cuts have also reduced the number of counselors and forced social workers and school psychologists to serve in many different district schools during their work weeks. Help for a potentially suicidal student may be delayed because the psychologist is working in a building miles away. As a result, when students need help, the help they need right now is often not available in the office of these designated helpers. Increasingly, these helpers are unable to deliver the intervention that is needed, given their limited ability to offer help.

Students understand this situation and look to other sources of help, such as angel teachers who operate quietly under the radar. In today's school communities, they are given top priority as the "go to" helpers. They operate like doctors in field hospitals in war zones. Like soldiers hurt in battle, teens come to angel teachers in droves because they know they can be seen quickly and given an antidote to lessen their fears and pain and a prescription for recovery. Even if troubled teens at first decide they don't need immediate help, they know where to go when trouble strikes again.

War zones exist in the lives of many teens. Maybe they are not being shot at with bullets and bombs, although some are, but they are victims of abuse that may come in many forms and can tear apart their hopes, dreams, and once-safe worlds. Sometimes a bullet wound in battle hurts less than a barrage of hurtful words or a slap across the face. Wounds in battle can be seen clearly. The blood and pain cannot be masked. But wounds suffered by teens, from harsh words to physical abuse, can often be masked, with one exception.

Angel teachers who know their students well can see the emotional pain in their eyes and demeanor, their desire to be left alone, isolated in their misery and denial, and their fears of having to return to the scene of the abuse when school ends for the day.

Many go home to the same abuse, endure being bullied on the school bus, suffer from being called derogatory names, or are unable to end a so-called romantic relationship that has led to unwanted sexual behaviors. Most teen problems don't get better without help; they get worse. Teens need a trusted adult who can pull them aside and say, "Let's talk. You look pretty shook up. How about 2:30 in my room? I'm not taking 'no' for an answer. We're in this together. I can see you need help and my guess is you know it too. Let me help you, today."

Angel teachers can help troubled teens get the help they need. They are not trying to supplant or take over the roles of the designated helpers in the school. They are not after a "super counselor" role in which they pretend to be experts on teen problems. They are simply answering a calling to be of service and do what is required when they see a teen in trouble. The reality they and their students face is that in many schools the helping roles of counselors, social workers, and school psychologists have been downgraded. Angel teachers are stepping into a helping vacuum created by an overburdened school bureaucracy.

The "counseling" role of school guidance counselors has taken the biggest hit. Counselors will tell you as much in private, off the record. They feel their counseling role has been compromised by taking on too many noncounseling duties and simply being unable to engage in the daily school lives of students, unable to get to know them and be helpful.

Many counselors express bewilderment at being a target of hostility from parents and community members because they are unable to offer more intervention to students. They feel they are being wrongly accused of choosing to spend their time scheduling students for classes, supervising the testing program, doing college admissions counseling, and abandoning their personal counseling role.

Many of these caring professionals feel angry, saddened, and betrayed because they simply can't deliver the kind of help they were trained to offer, even though the school's public relations promise just the opposite. They are boxed into a no-win situation, asked to accomplish a task but lacking the capacity to perform the task successfully.

While this candid assessment of the helping process in the schools has been given little attention, it should come as no surprise. Students know it. Counselors know it. Administrators know it. Teachers know it. At the onset there was a need for counselors to intervene and offer counseling, when large secondary schools, many with over 2,500 students, were being torn apart in the 1960s by student rebellion and the increase in drugs and personal problems.

Since then the counseling role has diminished further as counselors have been increasingly called upon to manage the bureaucratic aspects of these large schools. Their primary role now is to get students in the right classes so they can succeed, to help make sure students are prepared for mandated tests so both they and the schools score well, and get students into college, hopefully the most prestigious ones. These are all critical factors in putting a winning face on the schools' achievements and keeping the critics at bay.

Much of the counselor's role today then is serving as an arm of the school's public relations and political efforts to guarantee public support. This is clearly an important role amid today's growing public outcry for budget cuts but it's not a role that includes much, if any, personal counseling. Let's not pretend and sell this role to the community as a way to help teens with personal, academic, and well-being problems.

Organizational life being what it is, organizations tend to stay with what they know and use the same sales pitch year after year to define the helping process, even when the helping process has moved in a different direction.

The example of angel teachers finding their niche helping troubled teens demonstrates that people within the organization often change more than the organization itself. These teachers seek to have a direct impact on matters that touch their professional lives and they want direct participation and influence. They have the skills to lead, to help, and they are not content to be just foot soldiers. As angel teachers they believe that they and many other teachers serving on the front lines, not the "expert" helpers, have the resources and practical know-how to solve many of the problems in their schools, such as helping troubled teens.

While it is true that some counselors prefer a quasi-administrative role instead of offering personal counseling to students, because of their own interests in becoming administrators, many counselors would welcome the professional freedom to be involved with troubled teens by offering individual and group counseling. After being trained in graduate programs emphasizing the counseling of students as a priority, upon arriving in the school environment they find themselves in a role far different from their training, career aspirations, and personal and professional hopes and dreams.

Like angel teachers, they become counselors in order to help kids; but then, unlike angel teachers, many find themselves pushing paper and sitting in front of a computer all day. It's ironic that counselors, who were initially identified in the creation of large high schools in the 1950s as having the chief role in counseling students, have over time gradually lost or given up that role, leaving a vacuum now being filled by angel teachers and, unfortunately, a few messiah teachers, in 2012.

The one bright spot is that angel teachers often come to counselors when they need advice on intervening with a difficult student or finding sources of referrals for students in life-threatening situations. One of the assets of angel teachers is that they create natural allies with skilled counselors, social workers, school psychologists, school administrators, school nurses, select colleagues, coaches, club directors, student leaders and peer helpers, parent advocates, community health and mental health workers, and law enforcement professionals, all of whom they can quickly call into action when they need additional support for a troubled teen.

The angel teachers can thus offer a large dose of support when the teens they are trying to help face serious, often complicated, problems. This process of angel teachers creating a support group of natural allies forms a "circle of wellness" that can provide a cocoon of safety for kids in need.

Angel teachers recognize that they can't do their helping job alone. They need help, advice, and support as they face the failures that are sure to come. Often, intervening to help troubled teens doesn't work at first. Angel teachers know they need to revisit these teens often and look for ways to sell them on getting help. They must be willing to face the rejection troubled teens give them, get over it, and try again. There is no easy path to offering help to teens who need it but may not want it.

Their initial rejection, the first round of the intervention conversation, often comes across with a loud "no, not interested, get lost" remark or a passive "maybe later" reply. Offering help to troubled teens is like fishing. If there are no fish biting, you have to move your boat and try again.

Angel teachers are human. They understand that choosing to include helping teens in their job description can involve more risks than teaching an academic subject, risks that this book will describe in another chapter. They are aware of the need to provide an ongoing self-care regimen and strive to lead personal and professional lives that are well balanced. This regimen requires keeping their own health, well-being, and personal needs in good order. As in sports, they come into the helping process ready to play and give their best effort.

The dual role of subject matter and angel teacher has many demands. Helping teens is like walking a tightrope. It's easy to fall off. The angel teacher can make mistakes such as thinking there isn't a problem he or she can't solve or getting too involved in helping a needy teen and taking on the risky role, for both the teen and the angel teacher, of crossing professional boundaries, entering into too close relationships such as friend, substitute parent, or even lover.

The angel teacher role requires constant self-assessment, vigilance, and ongoing support and feedback from trusted colleagues. It's much the same as therapists do in making sure their intervention path is on the right course for both them and their clients. This approach helps angel teachers keep active a red warning light in their psyches that is ready to come on if they are crossing professional boundaries.

Angel teachers are not in the helping role for self-promotion, acclaim, or notoriety. They understand the boundaries and limits involved. They are not available twenty-four hours a day, seven days a week. They don't meet outside school. Their vehicle to connect with students is through face-to-face interaction in the classroom, hallways, cafeteria, and at student activities such as sports, dances, concerts, plays, and other club and extracurricular activities—places where teens congregate and hang out.

However, the vacuum created by the limits being imposed on the counseling aspect of the counselor's role has not only created and expanded the helping role for angel teachers but has also allowed the risky role of "messiah" teachers to emerge. As described in this author's book *Innocence Denied: A Guide to Preventing Sexual Misconduct by Teachers and Coaches*,[3] messiah teachers represent the flip, dark side of the angel teachers.

Messiah teachers, posing as helpers for needy students, are a danger to the well-being and safety of these students. They prey on students who have suffered many rejections and are in desperate need of adult contact. Messiah teachers are at-risk professionals who become too involved with needy students and take on the role of savior, parent substitute, friend, confidante, and even lover. They see themselves as the saviors of lost teens.

Often they are teachers longing for the admiration and relationships they did not have as children; messiah teachers lack the skills to know when they are crossing professional boundaries and limits. They lack that red warning light that alerts them that they are abandoning their helping role and instead luring needy students into destructive personal relationships that often lead to sexual misconduct.

These abusive acts can have dire consequences for the students, their parents, the teacher, and members of the school community who fail to properly supervise the messiah teacher and protect the needy student. Secondary school administrators are often overburdened and, as a result, messiah teachers can operate under the radar, without detection, until the damage is done.

These messiah teachers can be found at the fringes of the school community, often loners with little connection to colleagues and community members. They often seek out students who are lonely and adrift, looking for an adult who cares. These students, like the messiah teachers, lack the warning light that would tell them to flee from such relationships. These needy students have been isolated and have faced many rejections and abandonment for such a long period of time that they are willing to settle for any companionship, even if it offers danger.

Students looking for an arena of comfort because of negative changes in their family life, home situation, peer relationships, and so on, often look to teachers for such comfort. However, in searching for such an arena of comfort, students sometimes connect with teachers who are untrained in close and personal contact with needy students and are themselves troubled by similar issues in their own lives—deteriorating personal relationships, divorce, caring for ill family members, loneliness and isolation, disinterest and boredom with teaching, aging, and so on.

These teachers may be looking for an arena of life or a set of role relationships within which they can feel relaxed and comfortable, to which they can withdraw and become reinvigorated.

This pairing of needy students with untrained and needy teachers can be a toxic mix, a relationship that begins with good intentions and barrels into dangerous territory, a relationship that is observed by colleagues who choose to look the other way, gossip about the relationship, or lack the skills on how to intervene and confront and help the teacher and student.

In a sense, colleagues are also victims. They see the risky behaviors unfolding but do not act. Looking the other way becomes a pattern in a school community that is supposed to be building trust and caring. In the end everyone loses: the teacher and student, their families, colleagues, students who lose trust in teachers, parents, community members, and so on. Many of these cases could have been prevented with training, supervision, monitoring, and early intervention. The pain that resulted for all involved didn't have to happen.

The majority of cases of teacher sexual misconduct involve a consensual relationship between needy teachers and students that emerges out of close contact, often for a prolonged period of time. However, a small number of teachers are predators and use their position of authority to lure vulnerable students into unwanted sexual relationships.

The good news is that we have developed a beginning profile of educators who have the potential to be at risk to sexual misconduct. The data from these profiles should help us take the necessary next steps in developing training, supervision, monitoring, and intervention programs.

Here is an example of such a profile focusing on teachers who become involved in consensual relationships that lead to sexual misconduct:

1. The majority of teachers involved in sexual misconduct do not go into the profession to prey on students or become involved in inappropriate behavior. They are not predators or psychotics.
2. Sometimes teachers involved in sexual misconduct are star teachers and coaches. They are professionals who are involved in close contact with students through extracurricular activities and sports. Some are icons whose success as teachers and coaches has earned them positions of power in the school and community, a position that they feel allows them to ignore boundaries, rules, and regulations and become involved in risky behaviors without being detected.
3. Teachers involved in sexual misconduct tend to justify their behavior by believing that they want their victims to have a deep personal relationship, and sometimes sex, with someone who cares about them.
4. Apparently teachers involved in sexual misconduct easily avoid detection by colleagues and administrators who may in fact be aware of their transgressions but fail to take the necessary steps to intervene to stop the misconduct. People don't want to see it. The educational system doesn't want to talk about it; they want to cover it up.

5. Many teachers involved in sexual misconduct don't stand out from the crowd and appear to be normal people who lead normal lives.
6. Often the teacher involved wishes that someone had warned him or her early on about the slippery slope that can lead to sex with students. They wish that colleagues had warned and confronted them rather than looking the other way or accepting hard-to-believe explanations.
7. Colleagues and administrators need to intervene and help when they see teachers crossing boundaries.
8. Many of the teachers involved, and their families, experience great shame, guilt, and regret.
9. There is little sympathy among colleagues for the pain suffered by teachers who cross boundaries or for their families.
10. There is little awareness that crossing boundaries can happen to any teacher, given a combination of personal and professional setbacks. Rather, the teachers are seen as black sheep, out of step, and not representative of the vast majority of trustworthy teachers.

High school teacher Gary Jarvis provides probably the best example of what can happen when teachers become involved in close personal contact with needy students without adequate training, supervision, monitoring, and intervention. I became involved in chronicling Jarvis's story in 1993 when a *Newsday* headline caught my eye: "School Sex Abuse: Sachem High School Teacher Held in Case Involving Teens."[4]

Jarvis was a neighbor of mine in Blue Point, on Long Island. Although I did not know him personally, accounts by community members described him as a model husband and an excellent history teacher at nearby Sachem High School in Ronkonkoma, New York. But all that changed on June 24, 1993, when Jarvis was arrested for allegedly having sex at a motel with an underage student and fondling a fifteen-year-old student in a classroom. He was arraigned on a third-degree rape charge and a charge of third-degree sexual abuse, both involving students less than sixteen years of age.

His neighbors were shocked. This was not the man they knew in the community. Jarvis ignored boundaries and became involved in risky sexual relationships with students that eventually led to the loss of his professional career, scorn by colleagues and community members, hurt and personal damage to his victims, and humiliation for his wife and family.

Jarvis, who was married and without children, had been teaching in the Sachem school district for eighteen years. He was successful in the classroom and earned tenure and had a positive evaluation every year. He was not a predator. He had no police record of past sexual misconduct.

But, as Detective Lieutenant Robert Hoss of the Suffolk County Police Department said, "He was taking her to motels for sex. It was more than once or twice, maybe for about a year. He didn't drag her there."[5] There appeared to be mutual consent between Jarvis and the student, a needy teacher and student finding each other and acting out right in front of the community.

Jarvis's behavior presents the picture of an unsupervised teacher spinning out of control, not only risking taking a student to a local motel but, in June of 1993, allegedly fondling one of his fifteen-year-old students who approached him in the classroom seeking consolation because her parents were vacationing on her birthday.

Police said Jarvis began his sexual liaison in the alleged rape case around May of 1992. It ended, Hoss said, and "she didn't want any part of him any more and I think he was running around looking for her in the neighborhood. 'Did you see so and so?' The parents after a while realized something was wrong."

The father of the fifteen-year-old in the June incident said Jarvis had taken his daughter to lunch in the past and made inappropriate sexual remarks. After the first hug the first day of the alleged fondling, Jarvis asked the girl if their lunch date was still on and reluctantly agreed to let her boyfriend come. "And he said to my daughter, 'It is time for a hug as we are friends again,'" the father said. "She reluctantly went over to him, and was afraid about what would happen, but since it was a teacher she went over to him."[6]

After the second incident the daughter went to school authorities. The parents, on returning from vacation, called the police. School Superintendent James Ruck said that school officials initiated the investigation after a student approached the principal of Sachem High School South. Jarvis was suspended with pay and the police were called in.

The teenage girl Jarvis took to motels testified that they had intercourse and oral sex, which Jarvis videotaped and photographed during ten months in 1992, when she was fifteen and sixteen years old. Suffolk County District Attorney Deirdre Creighton said, "He became her confidant." In her testimony the girl described how she lost her virginity to Jarvis, a father figure "who gave me attention he didn't give to other kids." The girl had grown up fatherless.

On July 18, 1994, Jarvis was sentenced to four to twelve years in prison. According to Estelle Lander Smith, before imposing the sentence Suffolk County Court Judge Kenneth K. Rohl read aloud portions of letters sent to him by a Sachem schoolteacher and the superintendent of Sachem schools, urging prison time for Jarvis and saying his behavior had eroded public esteem for teachers.

"He has betrayed a public trust and has victimized young impressionable students," Superintendent Ruck wrote of Jarvis. An unnamed colleague of Jarvis asked the judge to make an example of him, saying, "This may in a small way help to lessen the loss of respect of parents and students for teachers."

Jarvis's case raises many questions and supports my profile of teachers at risk for sexual misconduct. For example:

1. Jarvis is seen by some students as a father figure, a confidant, who is easily available to offer consolation and support to needy students.
2. His relationship with the girl he took to the motel appears to be consensual. As Detective Hoss suggested, "He didn't drag her there."
3. His blatant acting-out behavior appears to go unnoticed by colleagues, administrators, and community members. He goes to the girl's neighborhood looking for her. He takes her to motels in the area. He videotapes and photographs the sexual acts. He hugs another girl in his class, takes her to lunch, and makes inappropriate sexual remarks.

Jarvis's behavior should have set off alarms for colleagues, administrators, parents, and community members. But there appears to have been an eerie silence, a looking the other way, as Jarvis plunged deeper and deeper into sexual misconduct and the margins of school life. Didn't anyone notice? Where were his fellow teachers? It appears that there was none of the supervision, monitoring, or intervention that Jarvis needed. Boundaries were being crossed all over the place.

And where was the training that might have helped Jarvis become aware of his own destructive needs and offered him a road map for help? Instead, as the letters to Judge Rohl suggest, the district's response was that Jarvis's behavior was an anomaly and out of character for Sachem teachers, suggesting that this type of behavior doesn't happen here. The message was that Jarvis was a bad apple and, once he was gone, all would be well again.

The message was also that we don't need to train our teachers on how to establish clear boundaries when they become involved in close personal contact with students who are looking for a father figure, mentor, confidant, or consoler. Unfortunately the only lesson learned in Sachem seems to be that the problem was simply about Gary Jarvis, not about the teacher training, supervision, monitoring, and intervention process. This kind of response helped create a climate in which more teachers can follow in Jarvis's footsteps. Things stay the same. The only difference is that Gary Jarvis is gone.

The case of Gwendolyn Hampton demonstrates that messiah teachers are not just men. Gender may not be as large a factor as supposed. Increasingly, reports of sexual misconduct in schools involve women educators. Of nearly 250 cases of alleged staff-on-student sexual misconduct reviewed by *Education Week*,[7] forty-three of them, or nearly one in five, involved women employees. In five of those cases the victims were girls. The rest were boys in middle or high school, ranging in age from eleven to seventeen.

Given such a female-dominated profession as education, such numbers evoke little surprise. However, we need to keep in mind that the possibility of teachers becoming involved in sexual misconduct is still repressed in many communities and the thought of women teachers involved in such behavior is denied. Many school professionals and members of the public believe that most educators would never even consider sexual involvement with a student and no female teachers would do so.

To the contrary, there are teachers who do think about possible sexual involvement with a student, and some of those teachers are women. To think otherwise is to deny such contact can exist and in the end leave teachers without necessary training, monitoring, supervision, and intervention. Therefore, in our work to rid schools of teacher sexual misconduct, we need to raise awareness that there are women educators who are at risk to sexual misconduct.

As Gwendolyn Hampton's case reveals, when untrained and needy female teachers become too involved with needy teens, misconduct can happen, misconduct that takes place right in front of administrators and teachers but is observed only by other students.

Thirty-two-year-old Gwendolyn Hampton earned respect as a seemingly devoted Spanish teacher, counselor, houseparent, and single mother at John Dewey Academy, a private boarding school for troubled teenagers in the small western Massachusetts town of Great Barrington. But students and staff at John Dewey said they felt betrayed by Hampton after a federal civil lawsuit alleged that she had a secret sexual relationship with a student, Adam Helfand, and had at least one child by him. The relationship continued after Helfand graduated from John Dewey and attended college.

Hampton said, "I didn't believe I did anything wrong. I feel I was good for Adam at the time I had a relationship with him. I certainly wasn't luring or enticing anyone." Helfand, who was expelled from an Illinois high school in 1999 for using drugs and alcohol, was supposed to be getting help for his problems at Dewey. Instead, he said, Hampton gave him alcohol and prescription pills.

The civil suit accused Hampton of "counseling malpractice." It alleged that Dewey Academy, its president, and its dean were negligent in failing to supervise Hampton. In her defense she said she developed a very close relationship with Helfand because she was asked to do too many things—teach him, serve as his primary counselor, and supervise him when he worked in the school kitchen. She often called him to her home to babysit or do chores and he became very close to her family.

"The boundaries were blurred; I was his lifeline," Hampton said. Even now, Hampton insists she did nothing wrong and cared deeply for Helfand. "I didn't see myself going out with a kid," she said. "I brought out the best in him. He made grown-up decisions, mature decisions."

However, a sense of betrayal lingered at the school, which was home to twenty-nine students, many of whom said their lives had been transformed by the program built on intense confrontational therapy. Matthew, a seventeen-year-old student, credits Hampton's counseling sessions with helping him give up his dishonest and manipulative ways and learn to tell the truth.

"I feel as if she was very hypocritical," he said. "She did something that is almost unforgivable, that is very dangerous for the school. She didn't think of the consequences of her actions. She never followed her own advice."

Diana Gittleman, a lawyer who taught part time at Dewey Academy, said that nobody had a clue. "It blows my mind because I think of myself as an intelligent and sophisticated woman," she said.

Hampton's behavior is consistent with our profile. She felt she was good for Adam and was helping him, not trying to date a kid or lure him into a relationship. But, as she reports, she became too involved as a teacher, counselor, and supervisor and formed a very close personal relationship with Adam. As the relationship evolved her own need for such intimate contact emerged, with Adam spending more and more time at her home babysitting and doing other chores. The boundaries got blurred. Mischief happened.

As her student Matthew said, she didn't think of the consequences or follow her own advice. Where was the supervision and monitoring by school administrators and colleagues? Clearly Hampton was crossing boundaries and heading for trouble. Hampton's students were aware of her relationship with Adam. During one of the weekly confrontational group therapy sessions at the school, where staff and students gathered in a circle, Hampton acknowledged being questioned about Adam's continuing visits after graduation and whether the relationship was appropriate.

She responded, "I said he was having a hard time adjusting to college and I was supportive of him, which was true." Where was the training for Hampton to serve as a primary counselor and adviser and lead confrontational therapy, to be a lifeline for Adam? Was Hampton prepared for the demands of close contact with a student who was ten years younger than she? How much counseling and advising experience and training did she have to prepare her for this role?

In the end she was charged with "counseling malpractice," suggesting that she either lacked effective training and counseling skills or chose to abandon them when her own needs became too powerful. Remember that Hampton was in her early thirties and Adam was in his late teens. In spite of the notions that "it can't happen here" and "no teacher should have such feelings," physical and emotional attractions can and do arise between teachers and students and can flourish without adequate supervision and intervention.

As this sad story reveals, it appears that Hampton was on her own, too involved in a close relationship, too needy herself, and operating without the necessary training, supervision, and monitoring to heed the red light of danger. No doubt she needed the confrontational therapy that students at Dewey had access to. Seemingly everyone was looking the other way except the students. According to Diana Gittleman, no one at the school had a clue, even when Hampton became pregnant.

Hampton falls into the category of what researchers describe as teacher/lovers, who fall deeply in love with the teenage student and need frequent validation from others. What you have is a needy child and a needy adult and, many times, that's just abuse waiting to happen.

One of the goals of angel teachers is to forewarn troubled teens to stay clear of messiah teachers and alert the school administration to intervene when they observe the messiah teacher crossing boundaries. Looking after the well-being of the students is part of the responsible role they have chosen.

There are then three major strands in our secondary schools that deliver help to students in trouble, but only one that is working well and that is the angel teachers. The other two, pupil personnel services—which includes counselors, social workers, and school psychologists—and messiah teachers, are failing to deliver the kind of help that is needed. Pupil personnel workers are overburdened and lack the time, energy, and support needed to get the job done successfully with the majority of students.

Messiah teachers represent the dark side of the helping process and are examples of what can go wrong when teens are unable to find safe and trustworthy open doors for help. They represent an open door to be avoided, to bear the label, "Danger. Enter at your own risk."

Angel teachers represent the students' best hope for help. They carry on their interventions quietly, with little interest in notoriety or stardom. In fact, that is why teens in trouble are attracted to them and line up outside their doors. Angel teachers are savvy about teen life, the problems they face, and how the helping process works.

Another aspect of the angel teacher role is that it is often chosen as a career alternative to avoid the stagnation and lack of novelty that visit teachers in their middle careers. By adopting a helping role in addition to their subject teaching role, angel teachers can find novelty, opportunities for new learning and skill acquisition, and risk. This dual teaching role helps them to avoid burnout and gives them renewed energy, spirit, commitment, and a way to build something new for themselves and the teens they are trying to help.

Building something new is an important variable in finding satisfaction, happiness, and self-worth in any personal or professional relationship. It's a critical component for troubled teens but also for teachers who seek a new career path without giving up their subject matter role. But in the beginning, building something new, as any carpenter will tell you, is a haphazard process without the experience one needs to do the job well. Trying to fit pieces together doesn't work and the final product sometimes looks like an amateur is in charge.

So it is, too, for beginning angel teachers. We all learn from good and bad experiences, mostly from the bad and our failures. It's often a rough road for beginning angel teachers but, with luck, they have mentors who can show them how the role works and how to proceed. It's a try this–try that approach until they find their way. Rome wasn't built in a day and neither are angel teachers. As managers in sports know, it's critical to be patient with rookies. Don't stomp on their dreams and hopes because of some failures. This is a lesson they can transfer to teens who are failing in their academic and personal lives.

Many angel teachers report they have chosen this dual role because they were helped by a caring teacher when they were troubled teens themselves. They have chosen to be helpers as a way to pay back the helping gifts they received, gifts of acceptance, encouragement, hope, support, and the necessary life skills to make their way out of troubled lives.

They create helping settings, often before or after school or at lunchtime in their classrooms, that have the following aspects:

- Welcoming and inviting
- Attractive, comfortable, designed for conversation
- Safe, private, trusting setting
- Well known in the school as a clear pathway to help
- Encourages teens to enlist and invite peers headed for trouble and to serve as peer helpers
- A setting where teens can find additional help and referral for highly risky behaviors—drug or alcohol addiction; suicidal thoughts; physical, sexual, or emotional abuse; bullying
- A setting that is respected and utilized by the designated helpers (counselors, psychologists, social workers, and administrators) and is seen as a legitimate helping arm of the school's intervention effort

Angel teacher Gary Smith is one of those teachers whose abusive home life led them to help teens who were experiencing abuse in their lives. They have a calling to answer the cries of troubled teens. It is the primary reason they chose teaching adolescents as a career and put in the necessary time and effort to learn about the problems facing teens and how to intervene, as described in the second edition of *An Administrator's Guide to Better Teacher Mentoring*.[8]

Here is Gary Smith's story of why becoming an angel teacher seemed such a perfect career choice for him.

Gary Smith had a dream and a calling to be a mentor for students. He had experienced many of the troubles facing his students and understood the risky territory of a fragmented family life—what it was like to be a frightened child—the lack of safety in the home, the abuse of a parent, no answer to one's cries for help.

But Smith also understood the need to fight back against abusers and develop a determination and the mental set to survive, to save oneself, and to be hopeful that things could change. He was successful in finding a way out of his own troubled home thanks to educators who helped guide him and his own desire to become a teacher, to do for other children what his teachers had done for him.

Mr. Smith was by all accounts the most popular special education teacher at O'Neil Junior High School in Deep River, Massachusetts. Many of the special needs students and their parents at O'Neil wanted Mr. Smith for a teacher. Smith taught a seventh grade self-contained class, which meant he taught every subject area except gym to twelve to fifteen students who had been identified as having learning, emotional, and sometimes physical problems that affected their ability to learn. Smith was with his students all day except for gym and made himself available after school for support.

Smith had special gifts as a teacher of the learning disabled. He had a reputation for helping students with a history of academic and social failures turn the corner and become successful achievers, with many going on to college. He had a 99 percent yearly passing average in getting his students to pass the Massachusetts Comprehensive Assessment Test (MCAT), one of the highest among special education teachers in Massachusetts.

Many students entered his class in September hampered by a variety of learning disabilities that served as barriers to learning and left in June filled with hope and a new confidence that they could succeed. But there was no mystery to Smith's success.

First of all, he worked very hard. He usually arrived at school by 6:00 AM with his bagel, coffee, and bag lunch. He was often the last teacher to leave the building, long after the extracurricular activities and events had ended. Smith was no eight-to-three, out-the-door-as-soon-as-the-last-bus-leaves kind of teacher. He made himself available after school to offer tutoring and support to his class and also served as a mentor to students in the regular academic program who were having academic or personal problems. Students and parents knew that he was available and his door was always open.

Walking the halls of O'Neil, one could hear students giving advice to their peers: "You should go to see Mr. Smith. He'll listen and give you good advice on what to do." No, he was not a professionally trained or certified counselor but he had a knack for helping kids who were heading for the margins of school life. Yet he seemed very humble, comfortable in his own skin, as the saying goes.

He was not looking to be a star teacher like some of his colleagues, who were into promoting themselves by lecturing at conferences and extolling how wonderful they were as teachers. Smith appeared not to need applause. His needs appeared to be simple: to demonstrate in every possible way that his students could count on him to help them navigate through their academic and personal problems and to listen to their hopes and concerns and use the information they shared to better understand his students and the family dynamics going on outside the school setting.

Smith had an extraordinary ability to store data about his students, data that he readily used to create a more personal relationship with his students and their parents. Smith was also available as a source of support for other teachers who were having teaching-related and sometimes personal problems. His door was always open and his colleagues, like his students, knew they could trust him with their struggles and get the help they needed to turn things around.

Needless to say, he knew every student in his class, and his knowing process was detailed and ongoing. I am not simply talking about remembering data like first names and IQ scores. Mr. Smith, as many of his fellow teachers said, really knew his students. He worked hard to get to know every aspect of their lives—home life, parents, siblings, home problems like abuse and divorce if they existed, abilities and strengths, hopes, dreams, fears, past failures, relationships with peers and teachers, health issues that could be getting in the way of school success, what made them laugh and light up or what prevented them from laughing. He seemed color blind, lacking in prejudices, and evenhanded in respecting and valuing each student. He didn't cultivate favorites or need to be worshipped by students and parents seeking his favor.

This is no easy task for a teacher, even one as gifted as Mr. Smith. He did his work without too much probing and without being too intimate. His listening, observing, and caring skills did the job. He noticed when students came to class with a bruise, a look of worry, or appearing anxious or out of sorts. He used simple words to help them talk and tell their stories: "How are you today? You've been absent for three days. That bruise on your face looks serious. Let's meet at lunch and talk about what's going on."

He used simple words and questions that teenagers understand and can feel safe in answering. In Mr. Smith they had someone to whom they could tell their personal stories and really be heard.

Yet Mr. Smith understood he was not his students' parent or friend. He was their teacher. His job was to ready his charges for the academic demands and tests they were facing until graduation, making sure they had the skills to navigate through an increasingly pressurized school world and pass the MCAT. But he also realized that he could use his teaching skills to help his students with their personal problems so they could become successful achievers.

He understood that his teaching role needed to include being an advocate and source of hope when dark times visited his students. Smith knew that every one of his students had experienced or would experience bad times. He was committed to being there for them but also realized that he couldn't make everything right or eliminate the emotional pains that come with life's problems.

He walked a fine line, caring for his students but at the same time understanding that they had families, sometimes troubled and imperfect ones, to go home to after school. He understood that he could not take on the role of a surrogate parent. He did what he could and he did a lot. His goal was to have his students leave class every afternoon better prepared to handle the academic and personal problems they faced.

In a real sense Mr. Smith was different from many other teachers at O'Neil. This is not a put-down of other excellent teachers but rather a realization that Smith seemed to have a special gift for keeping his students out of harm's way. His extraordinary ability to listen, tease out what was bothering his students, and help them resolve problems seems unique and special.

Early on in his career he appeared to possess an unusual gift for helping kids. It was as if he had years of training as both a master teacher and psychologist.

While there is something unique and special about Mr. Smith, his mission and desire to help each of his students didn't just happen. You see, Mr. Gary Smith, or Smitty as he was called growing up in Pittsfield, a small city in western Massachusetts, had a tough, abusive life as a child. His father, George, a logger for a local lumber company, came home drunk almost every night and took his alcohol-inflamed anger out on his wife Mary, Smitty, and his younger brothers, Mark and Jim. George created chaos and confusion almost every night, yelling about dinner not being ready, criticizing Mary's cooking, complaining about money and unpaid bills, and constantly bullying his three sons, telling them what losers they were. Smitty and his family never heard a word of love, praise, respect, or caring from George.

In spite of the daily terror, Mary was so intimidated by George that she could not allow herself to think about taking her children and leaving. In her mind divorce was not an option. A deeply religious person, she attended church every day to ask God's help in saving her children and finding a way out of their misery.

But her main reason for not leaving was her fear that George might kill or harm her and the kids, a threat he made often enough to paralyze Mary with dread. Taking the children and leaving could push George over the edge. So Mary, Smitty, Mark, and Jim tried to survive and hold on to the fleeting hope that maybe one day things would change. They kept looking for a crack in the door that would set them free from their lives of terror.

It was during those rough times that Smitty made up his mind not to allow this kind of abusive behavior to happen to other kids. He would study hard, play football, basketball, and baseball, win a scholarship to college, and become a special education teacher. This was a career in which he would be able to help kids with disabilities that needed fixing. In his junior and senior years he served as a mentor for peers in the special education program at school and was told by the teachers he had a gift for helping kids with special needs.

He would also help his mother and two brothers get free. He knew his father was headed for trouble with his increased drinking and poor health. Nothing could stop his self-destruction. Smitty was determined not to let his dreams be destroyed by George. If he became a teacher he could help other kids who might be going through the same turmoil he was experiencing. He understood that there were many kids with abusive parents like George.

He focused his mind and his will on a way out of his awful life and on his determination to resist George's baiting. George's ongoing put-downs of him for his good grades, sissy riends and the pansy decision to go into teaching—a field for women—were relentless. George knew no limits to verbally assaulting Smitty, even suggesting that his deciding to be a teacher was because he was gay.

Smitty fantasized about striking back, beating his father with his fists while he lay in a drunken stupor. Or even worse, plunging a knife into George's heart. It's easy to become violent and abusive yourself when you're constantly under attack. But he didn't. He studied hard, played sports, and got a part time job in the evening mentoring kids at the local after-school program; that kept him busy and out of the house. And he waited patiently for his time to come.

His determination paid off. He graduated third in his class and was accepted on full scholarship to the University of Massachusetts at Amherst. There he soon found great joy in learning to become a middle school special education teacher. He was, as one professor said, a natural. As he neared graduation Smitty felt a new confidence. He was free at last from his abusive home and on the road to becoming a teacher and helping kids survive their hard times. He hoped that his mom and two brothers would see that they too could find new lives and leave George to his own demons.

Gary Smith's troubled early life led him into a career as an angel teacher. He experienced first-hand the kinds of problems that can send most teenagers reeling—an abusive parent, too much responsibility in caring for other family members, and lack of help from the other parent, whose life was controlled by the threat of more abuse. But he had one thing going for him—going to school each day and finding opportunity and success.

Education was his ticket out of an abusive home. He forsook acting out and violent behaviors and channeled his anger and aggressive feelings into a life outside his home. In a sense, schooling saved him and helped make him into the person he became. Just think what would happen to teens like Gary if there were no schools to go to.

Smith's experience of finding a way out of his troubled family life is shared by many angel teachers. As a result they have learned how to look more closely at their students' behaviors and sense when they may be hiding problems in their personal lives. Because of their own experiences, they know that, even if teens have serious problems, these troubling times can yield a positive outcome if help is at hand. Afflicted teens can learn new life skills that will stand them in good stead when troubles again emerge in their lives. Angel teachers have a valuable teaching moment that they can use in sharing their stories with teens in trouble: if their teacher was able to find a way out of a troubled life, maybe they can, too.

The valuable helping role of angel teachers has for too long gone unheralded as a major tool in the school's intervention efforts, while the role of pupil personnel workers has been awarded far too much importance given their inability to deliver the help many students need. In all business interactions the prize goes to that group that can deliver the best product. The question raised in this book is not *who*—which group, department, or individual—should be involved in helping teens and identified as the organizations' designated helpers, but rather *who* actually performs that task successfully and is seen by the buyer—the students—as the go-to source.

In today's complex school life, what is listed on the organizational chart as *the* resource is often not the resource students go to when they need help. Any wise consumer listens to what is said on the grapevine, what relatives, friends, and neighbors say, before making a decision. Students are no different. They don't read or care about what is on the school's organizational chart and are not interested in how many degrees or years of experience the school counseling staff have. Deliverables and a "show me what you've got" attitude is what counts with teens, not the degrees, experience, honors, or books and articles written by educators.

For the angel teacher model to make a major difference, we need to expand the corps of angel teachers. We must encourage more teachers to take on the dual role of subject matter teacher and helper of troubled teens, and train them well for this important work. This book, then, is an effort to examine the role of angel teachers and make the case for school leaders to emphasize that angel teachers are key players in the school's intervention effort.

We have forgotten that the model for school counseling programs, the model of choice in most secondary schools, was established in the 1950s, after the end of World War II, over sixty years ago. Much has changed since that time and so have the problems of today's teens. Our secondary schools' intervention delivery system is in desperate need of a major overhaul and angel teachers need to be at the center of that overhaul.

Bill Gates, founder of Microsoft, offers the following advice on the need for an overhaul. Gates says, "America's schools are obsolete. They were designed fifty years ago to meet the needs of another age. Until we design them to meet the needs of the 21st century, we will keep limiting, even ruining, the lives of millions of Americans every year. . . . But these are our high schools that keep letting kids drop through the cracks, and we act as if it can't be helped. We designed these schools, we can redesign them. The basic building of better high schools includes making sure kids have a number of adults who know them, look out for them, and push them to achieve."[9]

Here is a series of questions that will guide us in making the case for angel teachers:

1. Why do some teachers choose to take on the role of angel teacher?
2. What are their skills?
3. Are some angel teachers "natural" helpers or is their craft honed over time with hard-earned experiences? Or both? Natural gifts supported by dedication, commitment, ongoing learning, training, and mentoring?
4. What are some examples of how angel teachers forge helping relationships with troubled teens?
5. What are the hazards and risks in the role of angel teacher? For example, why do some counselors, school social workers, school psychologists, colleagues, administrators, parents, and community members oppose this role?
6. How do angel teachers avoid becoming enamored of their special place in the school's helping hierarchy?
7. How do angel teachers avoid becoming messiah teachers and becoming too involved with needy students?
8. How do school leaders expand the corps of angel teachers so that quality intervention is easily accessible for students to meet their academic, personal, and well-being needs?

Secondary schools are the natural centers to provide intervention for troubled teens. Angel teachers are the professionals who can best deliver this help. It's no mystery that high schools, junior highs, and middle schools are where teenagers can be found each day and as such can provide education and community leaders a golden opportunity to help them redirect their lives when trouble visits.

Caring teachers who know their students well, look out for them, and encourage them to achieve are the winning ticket if intervention is to work in our large, often isolating secondary schools. The problem facing education leaders is that we need more of them.

NOTES

1. David Belcher, "Sheen's Circle, From Son to Father," *New York Times*, February 23, 2010, AR (1).

2. Wilborn Hampton, "Horton Foote, Chronicler of America in Plays and Film, Dies at 91," *New York Times*, March 5, 2009, sec. 6, 5.

3. William L. Fibkins, *Innocence Denied: A Guide to Preventing Sexual Misconduct by Teachers and Coaches* (Lanham, MD: Rowman & Littlefield, 2006), 1–35.

4. Eileen Yan and Robin Topping, "School Sexual Abuse: Sachem H.S. Teacher Held in Case Involving Teen," *Newsday*, June 25, 1993, 3 (A).

5. Estelle Lander Smith, "Teen to Testify at Teacher Sex Trial," *Newsday*, May 6, 1994, 25 (A).

6. Estelle Lander Smith, "Jail for Teacher in Student's Sex Abuse," *Newsday*, July 19, 1994.

7. Caroline Hendrie, "Abuse by Women Raises Its Own Set of Problems," *Education Week*, December 2, 1998, edweek.org/ew/vol-18/14women.h18, accessed August 13, 2004.

8. William L. Fibkins, *An Administrator's Guide to Better Teacher Mentoring* (Lanham, MD: Rowman & Littlefield, 2011), 203–7.

9. Bill and Melinda Gates Foundation, "National Education Summit on High Schools," February 26, 2005, 1–5, blogoehlert.typepad.com/eclippings/2005/05/bill_gates_amer.html, accessed October 25, 2011.

Chapter Two

The Kinds of Problems Troubled Teens Bring to Angel Teachers

Here is a series of vignettes that provide examples of the process troubled teens use to connect with angel teachers. These are not real people but serve to illustrate why and how students seek out help. In most cases they approach these teachers because the doors of the designated school helpers and school administrators were closed due to staff cuts caused by budget woes or staff were overburdened trying to contain the rising numbers of acting-out students and demands of the school organizational bureaucracy. Acting-out students who make the most noise and cause mayhem always demand attention and a response.

The school bureaucracy also demands attention and a response because it too makes noise, lots of it. It's an example of school politics at its craziest and is an ongoing nightmare for caring administrators who operate in a constant budget mode, keeping the lid on acting-out students and school critics so bad news doesn't destroy them, their staff, and their school.

As a result many troubled students are left to get help from angel teachers or they don't get it at all. The doors of angel teachers are often the only doors open to these students. Thank God we have angel teachers to fill the helping gap. These vignettes will illustrate why we need more of them.

Chapter 2

ADAM: THE "BAD" BOY WHO REALLY WASN'T

He had always been a "bad" boy as far as the school and his parents were concerned. Teachers labeled him as "sneaky," "can't be trusted," "troublemaker," "wise ass," and a kid to be watched closely. But he really wasn't that bad a kid. Yes, he was capable of making mischief but he was not a kid who was out to take on a teacher and destroy the class.

He just looked that way, couldn't help it, appeared as if he were a time bomb ready to go off and turn the class into mayhem. He was a teen who scared even the most secure teachers with his look. You know kids like Adam. They walk into a classroom and the teacher stops short, suddenly silenced, wishes that the counselor had made an error in placing this boy in her class, and prays he'll be gone tomorrow. Otherwise it's going to be a long, long year for her and him.

Adam had been on the watch list since elementary and middle school, so by the time he arrived at the high school, he had a dossier filled with minor offenses, detentions, and academic failures. The offenses were actually very minor—talking out in class, laughing out loud, no homework, cutting class, and smoking on school grounds—not serious acting-out behaviors, fighting, or challenging authority. He was just a kid who was interested not in academics, but only in hanging out and getting some fun out of life.

But he was on the list of kids to be watched and so he was as he moved from class to class. Unknown to his teachers and school administrators, by ninth grade he had decided to settle down and do well in school. He was tired of the routine of coming to school and being viewed as a "bad" kid. But he soon learned that getting rid of a bad reputation in school is not so easy. He had become "someone of interest" to his teachers and they focused on him as a kid capable of making trouble.

Reading the school records of new students can sometimes do more harm than good, as they may tell a story that is no longer accurate, if it ever was. Problems defined in elementary and middle school are often normal behaviors in high school, behaviors such as being late for class, talking out loud, not paying attention, lack of effort, etc. In high school these problems are dealt with on the spot by the savvy teacher—confronted, done over, forgotten—and not referred for counseling or a parent conference. The latter are actions reserved for serious behavior problems.

For upper grade teachers there is a need to be careful not to judge students like Adam before they are actually on the scene and can be observed face to face. Unfortunately this is not always the case. Those with the responsibilities of possessing, evaluating, and sharing information about incoming kids need to be careful about the negative impact of such information on newcomers. Information, as with all media, can be lethal even if forged with good intentions.

So, even as Adam tried to change, he was labeled as a potential troublemaker. He needed someone to help him figure out how to escape from the box he was in. He knew he had value but he seemed unable to convince his teachers of this. He was not the "bad" kid, ball-buster, or wise-ass kid he was portrayed as being. The middle school had made him out to be a "problem child."

His parents had gone along with this. They considered him lazy, on the road to dropping out and ruining the family's reputation after his older sisters had done well academically and were now in good colleges. Some parents side with the school when what they should do instead is give their teen sons or daughters some space and support and hold their breath rather than lowering the hammer and making their teens believe they are problems and failures. Often the offenses are minor at best and perhaps should be ignored rather than adding more fuel to the fire with negative words and penalties.

That wasn't Adam's story. But he moved on, on his own, and now wanted a new identity and place for a fresh start. He didn't care what his parents wanted. The change he wanted was for himself, his fight for a new beginning. But he couldn't do it alone. He needed an angel teacher to help him reverse the sentence, the label, that had been bestowed on him and let the new Adam take his place.

A name popped into his head as Adam was having this important self-discussion. A middle school principal had told him to look up Dave Gillespie, an English teacher at the high school, if he ever found himself needing someone to advise and help him. And so Adam's quest to find his path began. Sometimes a helpful suggestion from a busy principal does sink in with students even though their expression says, "No way."

Dave Gillespie was not surprised to find a new student at his door at the end of the school day. Many kids came to him for help with school and home problems. It was a role he enjoyed, giving him a needed break from teaching AP English to gifted students. As he talked with Adam he was intrigued by this kid's desire to be taken off the "most wanted" list and be seen as a good student. As an experienced teacher he realized how easy it was for students to be stereotyped as trouble makers. It was the way the school operated.

Some faculty members spent too much time talking about supposedly troubled kids but doing little to help them before their problems got out of control. They were left to say, "Didn't I tell you this kid was going to be trouble? Why don't the people in charge ever listen to us?" It's as if they saw their role as being a voice to warn colleagues but having no responsibility to reach out and help the students they were talking about. Their warning, stereotyping voices carried great weight in the school culture, adding to the growing concern of staff that more and more at-risk and troubled teens were coming up from the middle school.

Dave was not one of those teachers. He believed his teaching role included the mission to do something to help kids in need. He wanted to counter the notion that the school population included many troubled kids and the perception that the presence of these kids was damaging the academic reputation of the school. What Dave observed were some kids just being kids. They got into trouble for using poor judgment or having personal troubles that needed intervention. The students were not out of control, as some faculty members suggested. Dave's calling was to help these kids and confront faculty members who were constantly sounding the alarm about hordes of undisciplined kids roaming the school.

He understood Adam's dilemma and knew what to do about it. He told Adam, "I completely understand what's going on in your mind and I'm glad you stopped by. Here's what I'm going to do. I know all of your teachers on a first-name basis. They're good people. I'll speak to each one of them individually and ask their help in supporting your effort to succeed and be known as a well-behaved student.

"If you would like, I can call your parents and set up a meeting to give them a sense of what is going on with you. Of course, I want you there. I am also going to talk to Bill Borden, the school social worker, and ask him to support your effort and see you occasionally. Finally, let's you and I meet after school every Thursday—that's tomorrow, by the way—until you feel you've reached your goal for a makeover."

CHRIS: FINDING A SAFE HARBOR WHEN HE NEEDED IT

He would never forget the date and time and how it happened. It was Monday, October 15, lunch time. As usual he was eating alone. He was in ninth grade at McArthur High School, not doing well, failing every class except social studies. The social studies teacher, Mr. Schofield, was cool, a nice guy. But Chris hated the rest of his classes.

He especially hated gym, where the teacher, Coach Ryan, was always on his back because he never brought his gym clothes. Ryan never asked or seemed to even care why Chris didn't have gym clothes. The answer was easy: he didn't have the money and neither did his mom. He wasn't going to make her feel even worse than she already did, not having enough money to give her kids what they needed. He'd take Ryan's yelling and fail.

So here he was, sitting alone in the cafeteria, feeling very down after what happened at home last night, when he noticed Mr. Schofield heading toward his table. The teacher said, "Chris, good to see you here. Mind if I sit down? I see you brought my favorite lunch, peanut butter and jelly. By the way, I am so glad you're in my class. You've got a good mind and seem to enjoy it. But I understand some of your other classes aren't going so well, which brings me here today.

"I want to make a deal with you. I want to help you figure out how to turn things around. I'll get right to the point. I know what's going on at home. And I know I can help you with some of your school and home problems.

"Your mom called me this morning. She said you told her how much you like my class and thought I was the kind of person who could help you. She told me about what happened last night. She said there was a violent argument and your father hit her a number of times with his fists. She said he was drunk, that you tried to intervene and hold him back but he just shoved you out of the way. She said you ran next door and asked your neighbor, Mr. Toomey, to call 911. I guess the police came and took him to the station and locked him up. He's still there according to your mom.

"This must be pretty frightening for you, especially sitting here and seeing all the other kids laughing and seeming to have fun. But don't fool yourself; many of those laughing kids have home and school problems, too. I know because I am involved in helping some of them.

"So here's the deal. Let's you and I get together in my classroom right after school every Tuesday and Thursday. Tuesday is a time when you and I can talk and try to find some answers. Thursdays, Ms. Mulvey, the ninth grade counselor, and I meet with a small group of ninth graders with similar problems. She and I often team up to help them and I'd like you to join the group. They're great kids and they'll help you as well. Maybe you'll find some friends there.

"I also promised to keep your mom up to date, if that's OK with you. I gave her the name of a social worker, Ted Morrow, who works for the county. I know he will help her to figure out her next steps. I'm calling him to give him a heads-up on the situation.

"Look, Chris, we are in this together. You're not alone any more. Got to run. See you tomorrow; I am excited about having you join the group. And before I forget, I need you to give me permission to talk to your teachers about what's going on in your life. It might help them. And I want to talk to Paul Ryan about gym; he is an OK guy if he understands what's going on. And you may be eligible for free lunch; I'll talk to Mrs. Molder, the head cafeteria person."

Chris's life changed for the better that day. As Mr. Schofield said, he found his school "family" and support. He knew Mr. Schofield didn't have to sit and talk to him that day but he did. His mom's life changed for the better that day, too. She got help and a new job. She and Chris's dad divorced and for a long while it was sad around the house, but it all worked out. Chris's father attended AA but continued to struggle, but as Mr. Schofield told Chris, "It is what it is; we go on; we do our best."

KAREN: SHE'S ALWAYS COVERED UP

When walking the hallways of our large high schools, you sometimes notice a student who is perpetually overdressed, even on the hottest of days. Karen was one of those students—no skin exposed except her face and hands. No one knew that there were reasons she dressed this way, hiding her body beneath layers of clothes. She kept her story hidden from teachers and peers who were concerned about her isolation and lack of contact.

The look on her face always seemed to say, "Don't bother me, don't ask questions, don't try to be my friend or counselor, it won't work." She seemed a formidable figure whose message was, "Don't mess with me." And so teachers and peers didn't. They gave her a wide berth. They thought, "Why help a kid who is so secretive and angry when she doesn't want to help herself?"

Inside, she did want help but didn't know how to reveal herself, tell her story, for there was almost too much to tell, too many stories that were intertwined. She knew if she told her story there would be more hell to pay at home: more beatings, more work, more being a servant to her father and brothers. There was no hope of ever having friends, going to a dance, having friends over to her house for a sleepover, never mind the hope of someday getting out of the house, going to college, making a new life for herself. No hope that someday the beatings from her father would stop.

Karen's life work was sealed. She made the family meals every night, cleaned up, made lunches for the next day, did the laundry, took care of her sick mother—on and on until she literally collapsed into bed. But not until her father checked her "jobs," as he called them. If he found them wanting, he would take off his belt and beat her arms, legs and rear until she bled, all the time saying, "I'm doing this for your own good. You'll never find a man to marry if you continue to be so sloppy. A good man is always looking for a partner who can cook, clean, take care of him. That's the way it was when I grew up and that's why I married your mother. Until she got sick, she took care of everything, including me. You'll see I'm right as you get older."

Karen's resentment grew and grew. Her servant life was destroying her, as it had done to her mother, a once beautiful and vibrant woman who slowly gave up after years of beating and verbal assaults into being sickly and a recluse, committing suicide in her own way. Now Karen had taken on her mother's role and was being beaten down in the same way. Her father was the one who was emotionally ill and taking his sickness out on her mother and her. Her brothers were no help as they would never challenge their father's authority. Besides, they liked to be waited on and catered to.

But Karen wasn't going to end up like her mother. She knew the day would come when she couldn't take it any more, when she would fall apart and call for relief and help. She knew it would happen in school, in a place where she would be guaranteed a safe haven. It would be in Ms. Coughlin's business class. She knew Ms. Coughlin was concerned about her, but she wasn't pushy like some of the other teachers. She had a nice, easy, caring way about her. She would be the one to choose.

And that day arrived after a horrific night of beatings that left her bloodied and disorientated. She forced herself to get dressed and take the bus to school. Barely able to walk, she made her way to Ms. Coughlin's room and was relieved to find the teacher at her desk. She stumbled into the room and sobbed, "I need your help. Please help me. I'm in big trouble."

And then she collapsed. But help was on the way. Sometimes teens have to literally fall down so they can get the help they need. That's the only way they know to find a way out of their misery.

Schools may not be perfect organizations but they do play a critical role as a safe haven for teens in trouble. Angel teachers are often the core of this important backup system. It's not a mystery that troubled students like Karen know intuitively the angel teachers they can turn to when all seems lost. It's as if they check out each of their teachers ahead of a collapse so they know where they can get help, help from an angel teacher like Ms. Coughlin who, in her quiet way, sends Karen a signal. "I am here for you and when the time comes you can find respite, peace, and help here. Come lie down, rest, I will help you get well and get the help you need. I will take care of you now."

WHEN COACH REDDY DIED, THEIR WORLD CHANGED

There are times in adolescents' lives when a teacher they know well, admire, and count on for support dies. Sometimes it happens to a seemingly healthy, energetic, and upbeat teacher. Teens often feel they and their teachers, parents, and peers will live forever. After all, schools are all about youth, energy, risk, and taking on the world. Death and dying are distant strangers and seem to happen only to aging relatives or neighbors.

Often, protective parents shield their children from the death and the dying process, not allowing them to visit the hospital to say goodbye to Grandpa on his deathbed or attend the funeral and burial ceremonies. Parents think they are doing their children a favor but it robs them of learning how to act and grieve when a loved one dies.

These teens are unprepared when a tragic illness suddenly strikes someone they care about. This was the case with Tim Reddy, a teacher-coach who coached the girls' varsity soccer team, guiding them to the county playoffs. A few days before the playoffs he collapsed at practice and was rushed to the hospital. He had a brain aneurysm and was not expected to live out the week. The soccer players found themselves confused and angry that their best teacher-friend would no longer be with them on the field, giving each player the special support he was known for in the school and community.

Seeing Coach Reddy lying nearly lifeless on the field had put a sudden stop to the players' lives. Winning the championship, getting a college scholarship, or playing in an all-star summer league no longer seemed so important.

This was the kind of illness and imminent death that was not supposed to happen to him or them. In this kind of traumatic situation, with its painful finality, teens find they have to become adults real fast. They had to go on. There's no bringing the coach back and there's no longer the luxury of thinking death is something that will occur in the distant future. It's here, in the school, in the locker room, on the soccer field.

The death of a beloved teacher has a strong hold on teens. Their parents can't shield them from the pain and anger. New behaviors are called for—visits to the hospital, support for peers and themselves, sharing about the wonderful contributions made by the coach, and talking about how to handle the coming ordeals, the actual death, wake, funeral, burial, and getting back to whatever normal their new normal will be, gathering themselves for the playoffs.

The illness and death of a much-loved teacher became the center of the players' lives and issues like SAT tests, the prom dress, the prom, and graduation were suddenly sidelined, silenced. The players were getting ready for another type of fact to face and combat—being part of the death of Coach and wanting, yet not wanting, to be taken out of that horrific process even though they were frightened and unsure. They wanted to run away, go back to last week when all seemed so great, with the team celebrating winning the league title.

The team knew they had to come together, help each other through this dark time, and be an example for the other students. They knew that was what Coach Reddy would want for the team. In his pregame and postgame talks he often said, "This game isn't just about winning. Sure, that's important. But it's more than that. It's how we carry ourselves as people and the example we set for the other students. We're not brawlers, name-callers, dirty players, and we don't blame the refs when we get a bad call or lose the game. We play hard, fair, and, if we win, great. If we lose, so be it. We are not crybabies or whiners. We are in control of our emotions and our fates. You are so lucky to have the athletic skills and gifts you have. Be thankful each day to be able to enjoy each other and the game. I am."

So the team, still under the guidance and influence of the dying Coach Reddy, banded together, knowing the only path for them was to go on and stay on course.

When the news broke that Coach Reddy was seriously ill and had little chance for recovery, it seemed that everything just stopped in the school. Life as the students and staff had known it had changed in a day. The administration tried to get as much information out as they could and asked the teachers to share the information and encourage students to talk.

Reddy had touched many lives. Only thirty-five years old, he had been in the district for ten years, serving as math teacher and coach, and had developed a huge following among students, staff, alumni, parents, and community members. He was often mentioned as a possibility for becoming the next high school principal or even superintendent.

The announcement from the administration simply said Reddy was extremely ill and that the family asked for prayers but no visits. The students turned to each other and favorite teachers for support. The school literally shut down for a few days, allowing students and teachers to digest the impact of this event. But the students didn't really believe that Reddy would actually die. Surely God or a miracle would save him.

But by the end of the week his wife, Maria, asked that he be taken off life support. He died peacefully with Maria; his three sons, Mike, Jeff, and Bill; the school principal, Sal Alvarez; and assistant soccer coach Sarah Higbe at his side. It was left to Alvarez and Higbe to share Reddy's last hours with students and staff and hopefully provide some closure to them. Higbe was chosen to take over Reddy's coaching job and lead the team into the finals.

The wake, funeral, and burial took place, with buses being provided for students, who turned out in large numbers. A wall of tears filled each event. The team, students, and staff came together as one caring family, paid their respects, talked about all the great times with Coach Reddy, and hoped and prayed that he was at peace. And they offered their continued support to Reddy's wife, sons, and the new coach.

After the burial and further sharing, there came the time to go on. A new darkness had entered the students' world but so had a new caring and love for each other and what they had together. The death of Coach Reddy had left both the students and the staff feeling their own vulnerability and the need to take better care of each other. It was time to play the game and carry on what Reddy had built and worked so hard for. As he would have said, "It's time to hang tough and see what we're made of."

So it came down to Sarah Higbe to help the team and the school community move on, to live but at the same time grieve. Something awful had happened and as she told the team, "Your feelings are not going to go away, disappear, so be it. Don't fight your feelings. Do your best."

As Coach Reddy would often say about her, she had the right stuff. She was a winning combination of a coach, counselor, friend, and advisor, someone the players and students could relate to, talk to, listen to, and emulate. She was an angel teacher who arrived when one was desperately needed to help the team, students, and staff go on.

KRISTIN: THE TOO-GOOD CHILD

There are teens in our schools who are too nice for their own good: kids who are not taught to stand their ground when harassed and bullied by peers; kids who are raised to be nice, agreeable, turn the other cheek, and pray when confronted by a bully, pray that the bully will quietly go away and leave them be. They don't realize that bullies become even more aggressive when they meet no resistance. Bullies can sense terror in their victims' eyes, shaking hands, and muted voices, signs that give them permission to increase their assaults. Being too nice is like having a disease that can kill you unless it is treated.

Kristin was one of those too-nice teens. She was always smiling, dressed properly, an excellent student, vice president of her class, president of her church's youth group, and from a "good" family. She had successful parents who were active in community, church, and charitable organizations as well as volunteers at the local homeless shelter. They had raised their children to be kind and helpful to others regardless of color, economic status, and abilities. Kristin's mom, Ingrid, always preached that part of their responsibility was to lead peaceful lives and reject name-calling, self-promotion, jealousy, anger, and fighting.

Because she attended a small elementary school and then middle school in her neighborhood, Kristin had no problem with nasty peers. The schools were located in an upscale area and most of the students came from "good" homes. The school administrators could count on parental support and so no mischief was tolerated. The schools were like protective bubbles where kids were expected to be nice, get along, and model good behavior. Anti-bullying workshops for students, staff, and parents were offered regularly to encourage civility among the students. Both the elementary and middle schools had received recognition from the state and federal office of education for their outstanding efforts to prevent bullying.

But that protective bubble disappeared when Kristin went on to high school. Her parents had considered sending her to a private high school after hearing that the high school had a number of "problem" kids. But they felt Kristin should not be shielded from the real world; attending a school with a student population from different social, cultural, and economic backgrounds would make her more world-wise.

Kristin's experience in her new school proved to be just the opposite. Her first reaction to the school environment was fright. The school was housed in an old building, built in the 1940s, and housed over 2500 students. The classrooms, gym classes, halls, and cafeteria were crowded. To her surprise, fistfights and screaming fights among male and female students broke out on a daily basis. Police officers were stationed in the school to maintain order but that didn't seem to stop the fights. Some of the students belonged to neighborhood gangs and brought their gang battles to school.

Kristin knew few of her classmates. Many of the students from her old school had opted to attend private schools. She felt alone and isolated. She didn't share her feelings of fear and isolation with her parents because she didn't want to appear unable to meet the challenges that this new school offered. She had never been a quitter and didn't want to give up now.

In spite of her resolve she came to school each day frightened and confused. She wondered what kind of a crazy place she had come to. Why was there so much fighting and chaos? Weren't there any other kids like her there? Then, one day in late September, things got worse.

While changing in the locker room for gym, a group of girls surrounded her and started to call her names, some she had never heard. She began to cry and felt like she was going to faint. They kept it up, chanting, "Nice, pretty mama's girl don't belong here. This is our school. We rule. Get your f'ing self out of here and go to one of the private schools in the suburbs."

Just when she thought she would pass out, the gym teacher, Marty Blair, walked in and said, "What's going on here? Everyone else is dressed and in the gym. What's the hold-up?" No one said anything but Blair could read the scene. The group was targeting Kristin, trying to intimidate her, and, as Blair could see, they were succeeding. Blair said, "Okay, everyone out of here now but I want you to stay after class. I don't allow this kind of behavior in my class or locker room."

After class they all sat in Blair's tiny office. He said, "I'm not asking you to tell me what happened. I know. You were picking on Kristin, right? That's stopping right now. The next time it happens we're going right to Mr. Griffin's office and I'll make sure you're all suspended. Got it? You want trouble, you'll get it. And believe me, everyone in this school knows I don't tolerate this bullying crap. Try it again and I'll make your life miserable.

"I've been a teacher for twenty-five years so I know a few things about how to handle this gang stuff. And I know some of you girls are trying out for my basketball team. Don't count on making the team unless you show me you can get along with other kids and be a team player. I don't care how much ability you have. If you lack the ability to share and get along, see you later. Is this a threat and a warning? You bet! This gym is my home, my territory. Don't ever come in here and think you own it. Big mistake. That's it. Let's begin turning this around before I have to really intervene. Kristin, I want you to stay here a minute."

And so Blair took on the role of helping Kristin to toughen up. She told him how lonely and unprepared she felt in the new school. How she didn't know how to be tough or fight back. Blair understood but realized understanding was not enough. He had to give Kristin a tutorial on how to handle bullying types of behavior that were all too common in the school, how to develop a voice, body stance, and demeanor that said "back off, butt out."

The best way to do that was to invite Kristin to join the basketball team. He didn't know if she could play but he would use the game to teach her how to be aggressive when necessary, get help and support from teammates, and find a way to break loose when covered too closely.

So Kristin found a home, a niche, in a school that appeared to offer no safe haven. She found it because she was confronted in the school-home of an angel teacher, Marty Blair. He was able to offer her the gift of how to survive in a tough world, something her parents wanted for her but didn't know how to deliver. They were good people but maybe too good. They needed a Marty Blair to teach their daughter how to protect herself from the dark side of life.

It's better to learn those skills as a teen than lead an adult life being bullied in personal and professional relationships. Schools can offer parents and students anti-bullying workshops every day but nothing works as well as having a skilled teacher like Marty Blair involved. He knew how the bullying game played out and how to stop it, things not taught in a workshop. One skilled angel teacher can stifle a great deal of bullying.

ERIC: THE STANDARD BEARER FOR TOO LONG, BREAKS

He had been the first in his class starting in preschool. School work always came easily for him in grade school. There was no pressure on him, not from himself or his parents. It was something he really enjoyed, learning new things and hanging out with smart kids. But in junior high school things began to change. There was a new kind of pressure on him that came with being bright. He had suddenly become a "somebody," a "local treasure." He had a new life filled with awards, going to special programs and camps, and seeing his picture in the local paper. He was the valedictorian in junior high and seemed a shoo-in for that honor when he reached high school.

Eric was the pride of his school and community, which was going through tough times due to the slow economy. The unemployment rate was over fourteen percent and rising. Two large companies that had employed many of the town's citizens had moved, leaving behind despair. Crime was up and so were family problems, addictions, and even suicides.

Eric represented what was good about the town. He was hard working, honest, and seemingly a friend to peers from every group in the school. There was no hubris to be found in this kid. The town's citizens were proud that Eric would no doubt be selected to attend an Ivy League school, Harvard or Yale or maybe MIT. While times were tough, they could point with pride to one of their own and his achievements and feel that something was going right, a local treasure flowering amid many failures.

That all fell apart in the spring of Eric's junior year. He was enrolled in four advanced placement courses in the high school along with taking two college-level courses at the local community college. Plus he was in the throes of visiting colleges. It suddenly became too much for him. All he wanted to do was, as he said, "make it stop, make it all go away." It had become too much, always being first, the standard bearer, and never having the chance to just *be*, be unprepared, fail, not always have to be the one with the right answers. He just shut down.

Eric's changed behavior was noticed by Dr. Francine Murray, his AP Social Studies teacher. Francine Murray had been teaching the best and brightest students for over twenty-five years. She understood the pressures put on bright students by themselves, parents, family members, peers, staff, administration, and community leaders.

As she often advised her students in one-on-one sessions, "Being bright has its downsides. Be sure to take good care of yourself. I am here to help if things get too pressured. Don't keep your feelings to yourself. Being a teacher for twenty-five years, I've heard it all. Trust me. I know how to help you if problems arise."

She took Eric aside after class and said, "Sit with me for a while. I know you have another class with Mr. Shapiro. I'll let him know I asked to talk with you. Look, I know you well and have a great deal of respect for you. I also know you are taking a heavy load of courses plus you have all this college pressure building up. I noticed you've looked tired and anxious for the past few weeks, like school isn't fun anymore. It's become a chore, a job that never ends. Am I right? Talk to me."

And so he did. "I just ran out of gas. I was tired of being number one and always in the spotlight, kind of like a wonder boy who can do no wrong. I realize it's not fun anymore. When you're a kid in elementary school, it's fun because there's no pressure. But in junior high and high school, things build up. Because you're bright and do well, there's always another hill to climb, another more advanced course to take, another scholarship to apply for, and another special program to attend. You're not a kid anymore. You're made into a mini-adult to represent the school and community. And you're expected to achieve and succeed, be famous, because you've always done it that way.

"But after spring break I just couldn't go on no matter how hard I tried. Something was telling me to stop before it was too late. If I keep going on this path, there will be no respite, no peace. When I go to college it will be more of the same and even higher expectations. I have to stop, now. It's the only chance I have to be a kid before I enter the adult world. I talked to my parents and they're naturally upset but OK with what I decide.

"Maybe you could help me to figure out how I can change this crazy path I'm on. I'm shaking all the time, you noticed, and I can't sleep at night. I'm confused and scared. All my friends are asking me what's wrong but I don't know what to tell them. I don't care if I'm valedictorian or go to Harvard. I just want this monkey off my back. Please help me. I'm so glad you asked me to stay."

Francine told Eric, "The answer is simple. Let's think about having a meeting with your parents and Frank Testa. In my opinion Frank is one of the best counselors we have and he has helped a lot of kids like you. I don't see any reason we can't reduce your course load. You don't need to be taking four advanced courses. Maybe you can opt out of the community college courses. And maybe you can put aside the college search for a while until you get a little less pressure in your life. You know you can always start off at the community college after graduation, or even take a year or two off to consider the best next step for you.

"Let's stop this rush to succeed. This discussion begins a 'time out for Eric.' I know Frank Testa and I working together as a team will be a big help to you and your parents. Once we have a plan, we'll pave the way for you with your teachers and help you plan what to say to your friends, who are rightly concerned about you.

"Let me stop now and go to see Mr. Testa. I'll ask if he can see you right after school today. We're in this together, Eric. Check back with me after lunch. I promise there will be better days ahead. This is the first day of your new life."

RENEE: BEWARE BEING THE CHILD OF THE TOO-GOOD PARENTS

Sometimes it may be better for teens to have bad parents. Sounds kind of weird, doesn't it? But for some teens it's true. They know what they're getting—not much. They learn early in life that they're on their own. They know it's up to them to make it out of their misery because no one is going to do it for them. They can't pretend that their parents are not bad people and, once they stop drinking, fighting with each other, and get a decent job, things will be fine. That never happens. They know their lives are not like those of other kids and the sooner they understand that, the better off they are.

The too-good parents can be more destructive to their children. They're the types that are always looking out for what's best for their teens, what is the right path to success, happiness, and the good life. For their teens they decide what to wear, the choice of friends, courses to take, the best teachers and counselors, what activities to participate in, what vitamins to take, when to go to bed, when to be home after the dance, what and when to eat, what college to attend and major to choose, what future career to consider, and, most important, how to avoid drinking, drugging, smoking, and damaging your reputation by hanging out with the wrong crowd.

The too-good parents are always seated in the front row at parenting workshops, asking, "Where are all the parents who could really use this workshop? Why are parents who are concerned about their kids the only ones who show up? It's a disgrace. No wonder their kids act out, fail, do drugs, and are headed for dropping out. We have an epidemic of parents who don't care about their kids. Thank God we're not like that."

It's a never-ending assault of "goodness" and "should" under the pretext of taking care of their children. "As a parent my primary job and responsibility is to look out for my child in this dangerous world we live in. I never had parents like that and I missed out on a lot of opportunities, like going to college. I am making sure my son/daughter doesn't miss out like I did."

The too-good parent always has a list of things to consider and do for their teenager when they arrive in the kitchen for breakfast and, in the evening at the dinner table, they want, demand, answers to "How did your day go?" "How are your teachers?" "Did you pick up your SAT application?" "Did they suspend those kids who were caught drinking at the dance?" "I heard that John was accepted at Harvard. I think your grades are better than his and you have many more activities than he." "Are you feeling OK? I noticed that you look tired this morning and you didn't take your vitamins."

Their queries are designed to make sure their teens are not getting into mischief, hanging out, wasting time, or beginning to question the wisdom of their too-good parents. The too-good parent wants to know everything about the child, twenty-four hours a day, seven days a week. The statement "They're too involved" doesn't do justice to the social environment and controls they create around their children so they don't get hurt, suffer failure, or get stained by troubled peers.

It's a process of indoctrination that makes the children of too-good parents fragile, vulnerable, and at risk to failure because they learn early to go along, not think for themselves, do as they're told. The problem is that along the way they stop thinking for themselves. The voice they hear in their mind is their parents', not their own. They've lost it by the time they reach junior high.

That's what happened to Renee. Her parents, particularly her mother, were always in control of her. She couldn't resist her mother's pressure and influence. Her mother was everywhere, squeezing every breath out of Renee's mind and body. It was always the same approach.

"I was thinking about your future, as I always do, and I think you should apply for the Rotary Club's exchange trip to Russia this summer. I know you'd rather stay at home but it would help make your record look so great. I picked up the application from Bill Fogarty, the club president. He thought you'd be a shoo-in for the award. Dad's being in the club won't hurt."

When Renee heard the familiar words, "I've been thinking about your future," she knew it meant one more responsibility was going to be added to her "to do" list. Her mom always had the final word. That is, until Mike Weber came into Renee's life.

Mike was one of the funniest kids in tenth grade, a carefree, free spirit whose main role in school was to make his peers happy. He was the kind of kid who could make fun of his teachers and peers in a way that wasn't demeaning or challenging. He was very active in the drama club, playing one of the lead roles in that year's play. He met Renee, who had joined the club as a stagehand. They soon became close friends and, in a few short weeks, girlfriend and boyfriend, a couple.

Renee found she could talk to Mike about everything in her life and the pressures she was under from her mom. Mike was a good listener and suggested to Renee that she talk to Gloria Withers, the drama coach, about her mom's pressure.

Renee's life began to change when she met with Ms. Withers. Gloria Withers knew right away what Renee was going through. She, too, was the victim of a too-good parent who told her, "I just want the best for you. I don't want you joining the drama club and hanging out with all those weird kids with colored hair and pierced ears." Gloria learned that when her mother said "the best for you" it was really for her mother, not for Gloria. She had secretly joined the drama club in school and was now a drama coach herself.

As she told Renee, "Mothers are not always right. Sometimes they care too much." Gloria suggested to Renee that it was time for her to begin breaking away from her mom's influence and begin to decide what she, Renee, wanted. Gloria pointed out that Renee's mother was not a bad person but was probably trying to make sure Renee had opportunities that were denied to her as a child. Gloria recommended that she and Renee meet with her mother and begin the work of turning or, better, returning Renee's decision making to her.

Gloria warned Renee that this was not going to be a walk in the park. "This is not going to go down easy for your mother. There will probably be fireworks between her and me and, of course, you. She'll probably feel you betrayed her and tell me this is none of my business, accuse me of acting like a counselor. But that's OK. We—you and I—are challenging her role and she has to fight back, get it out, before we can really talk. But I'm confident it will work out.

"I'll call her tonight and ask her to meet with us later this week. Now understand, she'll probably start questioning you about why I called. Simply say it's about a future role you might play. Which, in a way, is true. Hang tough, girl! And keep talking to Mike. He's a gem, that guy. I could use a hundred more like him. Hey, he brought me you.

"You know, your story is the theme of many Broadway plays, the search and battle for one's own identity. Maybe we could do a play with you and Mike in starring roles. You know, good guy helps girl change her life?

"By the way, I'm going to give Marge Holovak, the tenth grade counselor, a heads-up about our meeting with your mom. Marge has a lot of experience with this kind of problem and she'll back us up if your mom starts to overreact. You might want to consider seeing Marge yourself once we get this process rolling.

"You know, this is not just about helping you. It's also about taking the load off your mom. She probably doesn't see it but she is spending most of her life dedicated to helping you, even though it seems to me you can handle your own life if left alone. Your mom's control has not made you a weakling, not yet anyway, and you seem to want help in learning how to take her on and save yourself. So in the long run this may help your mom to become aware that she is giving up much of her life; she has no life but you.

"Clearly she is a bright and active woman and with help, maybe counseling, she too can find a new path in which she, like you, decides what she wants for herself, not smothering her own growth and development by always being of service and help to you. That's something my mom and I found out after many battles. We're friends now and talk almost every day.

"It won't be easy but it's a necessary battle. Maybe your dad can get involved in therapy as well. You haven't mentioned him once in our conversation. It appears to me that he's not really involved in your life and lets your mom handle things. Maybe she pushes him away and keeps him from sharing the parenting role? Or maybe he's not interested and leaves all the parenting stuff to her? In any event, it's time to call him on why he is relegated to the role of absent dad."

BILL: SHE LOVES ME, I THINK, BUT SHE DOESN'T PROTECT ME

Being safe, secure, nourished emotionally and physically, provided with hope and optimism, and encouraged to follow one's dreams are the cornerstones of effective parenting and raising a happy child. Some lucky kids get the full one hundred percent treatment. Most kids receive just a little of each, but just enough to move on and become successful adults. But there are kids like Bill who don't receive much, if any, parenting. Over time, they learn to become their own parent, until, if they're lucky, some caring adult enters their lives.

Bill was one of those teens. His birth parents had divorced soon after he was born. He never knew his father; the family story was that he was an alcoholic and had moved on to California. Bill's mom, Rhonda, was a heavy drinker and had the bad habit of getting drunk at local bars and bringing men home, men who were often alcoholics themselves and prone to violence and abuse. They often beat Rhonda and scared Bill into calling 911 to protect his mother and himself.

For much of his early life this was his routine, particularly on weekends. During the week Rhonda would tell Bill how much she loved him and promised she would change, stop drinking and bringing men home. But she never did. Bill tried to convince himself that maybe someday she would change and that hope kept him going through elementary school and junior high. He kept his anger toward his mother in check; he loved her and felt he had to stand by her so she didn't get hurt or die from some of the beatings.

Bill became the parent, the savior; he knew he had to be strong and vigilant, be the man. Meanwhile, he did OK in school but kept his problems to himself. He didn't want any teacher or counselor finding out. He worried that, if they did learn what was really happening in his home life, the authorities might put him in a foster home. He had seen that happen to some other kids in his neighborhood. He needed to protect his mom. He knew she would be at greater risk without his being there to protect her.

Things became worse when Bill reached high school. During the fall semester of ninth grade, Rhonda took in a full-time lover named Paulie. She told Bill that Paulie was a good man and needed a home while he was divorcing his wife. He had a good job in construction and would pay rent. But Paulie was a big drinker and, once he settled in every evening, it became a never-ending drinking bout until Rhonda or Paulie passed out or got into a major fight, usually over which of them had drunk the last beer.

Drinking wasn't the only problem Paulie had. He made it clear early on that he was in charge of the house and Bill had better go along. He told Bill, "I'll beat the living shit out of you if you start wise-assing me. I'm not in construction for nothing. Maybe I'm not too smart but I can deck anyone who gives me a hard time. Got it, kid?"

Rhonda became increasingly agitated and scared by Paulie's behavior and verbal attacks on her and Bill. But she kept telling Bill that Paulie was a good man, even though he had "some faults," and that Bill should just stay away from him.

Bill couldn't let go of his anger and fear. He knew that his anger toward Paulie was almost out of control. He knew he needed help before he did something stupid, like using the knife he kept hidden in his room. He feared he might have to kill Paulie some night when he was drunk and passed out.

So he did something he had promised himself he would never do. He told someone in school about what was happening, before it was too late. Bill sensed Paulie was capable of murder, particularly when he was drunk and out of control.

The someone he chose was Brad Phillips, his technology teacher. Brad had taken notice of Bill because of his computer and writing skills. Bill seemed to have a natural talent for writing and editing stories about the lives of teens in trouble. Brad sensed that Bill's own life experience might have spawned such awareness and that he might be leading an abused and risky life at home. So when Bill approached him and asked to talk, Brad was not surprised. Nor was he surprised by the depth of the problem Bill was experiencing at home.

After talking for over two hours, Brad said, "Bill, I am so glad you picked me to talk to. I'm honored. You're right. This is an explosive situation and we need to protect both you and your mom. Yes, she's probably going to be upset that you asked for help but over time she'll come to realize that it had to be done. You had no other choice. You're just a kid. You can't win against an experienced bully like Paulie or solve your mother's problems.

"But there are people who are trained to do just that. Come with me; we're going to talk to Martha Dixon, the student assistance counselor, and Frank Middleton, the assistant principal. You're not going home until we know it's safe there."

And so help began, thanks to angel teacher Brad Phillips. Frank Middleton made immediate contact with John Phelan, a colleague at the department of social services, who said he would make a personal visit to Bill's home accompanied by a police officer. Based on Bill's story, they would give Paulie the choice of leaving immediately or facing abuse charges. He also said he would tell Rhonda that she would be required to seek mental health treatment or be charged with child neglect and child abuse.

He told Frank Middleton, "I'll be at your office by eight tomorrow morning to let you know where we stand. My advice is to connect Bill with a family where he can spend the night. I don't want him going home. I'll tell his mom he's OK."

Frank called Tom Murray, Brad's team partner, asking him to take Bill home for the night. His son Dan was in many of Bill's classes. Brad told Bill, "I know you're scared but this can't go on. Your mom and you both need help, now. By tomorrow we'll know how our intervention is turning out."

The story took a turn for the better, although not perfect. Paulie didn't waste any time leaving. It turned out he had a prior record of abuse and other altercations with the law. One more strike and he was prison-bound. Rhonda did get involved with counseling and alcohol rehab but never could shake her addiction to alcohol and risky relationships with troubled men.

For Bill, the intervention gave him a source of support with Brad, Martha, and Frank and a friendship with Tom Murray and his family. He found a new family and came to realize he loved his mother but couldn't be her caretaker or savior. He had to save himself.

CHRISTY: I WANT TO TELL THE TRUTH BUT I'M AFRAID TO

She had been ill since childhood with a bladder problem, a problem that required ongoing surgeries for her to function in school. Now a teenager, she was about to have her tenth surgery. She was tired of it all, tired of being ill. She wanted to be normal, like other kids, instead of having special arrangements, like using the bathroom before and after every class and sometimes during class. She knew the other students noticed that she was "different" but they seldom pressed her to share what was wrong.

When some peers asked why she was in the bathroom so often, she told them it was a minor problem that was getting better. Long ago she had chosen to keep her illness a secret, thinking that, once she told someone, they would always be asking questions. "How do you feel?" "When is your next surgery?" "When are you coming back to school?" "How are you holding up?" Christy knew from experience that, if she told the truth, the other kids would label her as a "patient" who was always in need of support and cheering up.

Christy didn't want any such intrusions. She had more than enough on her plate just dealing with her illness and the ongoing surgeries. It took every ounce of energy she had just to keep doing what she had to do. She just wanted it all to go away, so she could just be a normal kid who didn't need to spend her days urinating in the bathroom. She knew some of her peers could be cruel and abusive if they found out and feared that they might make insulting jokes or comments about her condition, such as "Christy is pissed off" or "Christy is such a pisser." There was already enough gossip about her being "different."

She wasn't going to give anyone more ammunition that might make her a target of laughing and jokes from the school bullies who were always on the alert for new, vulnerable victims.

Hal Butler, Christy's social studies teacher, sensed her unease and discomfort. He had checked with Sandi Ryan, the school nurse, about Christy's health and learned about her ongoing battle with the bladder disease. Sandi filled him in.

"Christy keeps everything to herself. She asked me not to let any of the kids know. However, her mother came to school just yesterday and asked me to let her teachers know more about her condition and to help her in any way. She's worried that Christy doesn't have any support in school and is depressed over having another surgery in two weeks.

"You're here at the right time because, if anyone is going to break through to Christy, it will be you. I've seen you help so many kids and I know you have what it takes. I'll let Christy's mother know you're on board to help her. Go to it, Hal. Keep me informed on how it goes. I'll alert her other teachers and Jack Ryan, the ninth grade counselor, about your efforts, as well as Ned Mayo in the principal's office."

After a few hours of doing his homework about Christy, Hal sensed his approach to Christy would be a caring but firm confrontation, simple and to the point. The next day Hal asked Christy to remain after class. He didn't waste any time with small talk.

He started off the conversation by saying, "Look, Christy, I asked you to stay because I know about your medical problem and I want to help you. I understand your mom was up to school yesterday and asked Nurse Ryan to get your teachers involved to help you, too. She said you seemed depressed at home. I also understand you have a surgery coming up in a few weeks and you'll be missing a week of school. After talking with Nurse Ryan, I am sort of taking the lead in helping support and guide you.

"Sure, you can try to go it alone, but there comes a time when we all need support in how to handle our problems. I believe now is the time for you. Let me help you. Let's start with you telling me about your illness, the surgeries, and how you are managing your life in high school. I know a lot about teenagers and their problems."

With angel teacher Hal Burton's quick intervention, the burden was lifted from Christy's shoulders and was now shared among her teachers, school nurse, counselor, and principal. And the burden was lifted from her parents' shoulders; they knew they could now count on a team effort to pay attention, guide, offer support, and teach Christy new skills in order to cope with her illness in the school and home environments.

As Hal Burton told Christy, "We all have problems—some health, some academic, and some personal. We need each other to help us get through the obstacles and problems that have arrived in our lives. Finding a way to let others know about your problems will help them to do the same when life gives them a jolt. Think of yourself as a teacher, teaching others about you and your life. No, not everyone will appreciate your openness but many will, and they will be helped by your example. As a return, you will begin to feel less alone and more affirmed and hopeful in taking the risk to share yourself."

MY STORY

Teenagers in need, such as Adam, Chris, Karen, Kristin, Eric, Renee, Bill, Christy, and Coach Reddy's soccer team, can be found in many of our secondary schools. They come to school with great needs and in many cases they are helped by angel teachers such as Gillespie, Schofield, Coughlin, Higbe, Blair, Murray, Withers, Phillips, and Butler. No, the stories of these students' battles to lead normal lives are not found in their guidance folders or acknowledged at their graduation ceremonies.

Nor are the successful interventions of these angel teachers found in their observations records or acknowledged in the school districts' recognition of outstanding performances by district teachers. Rather, their stories are well known among appreciative students, parents, counselors, and school administrators, all proud that when help was needed it was delivered on time.

Many teachers go into education to have a career helping troubled teens just as they were helped by a favorite teacher. I am one of them, an example of a troubled teen who found his way to becoming a successful educator. Here is my story of how I was helped by angel teachers and coaches who saw in me something worthwhile and worth saving. It is a reflection that can be found in *Teen Obesity: How Schools Can Be the Number One Solution to the Problem.*[1]

I can relate personally to the hurts that can happen to overweight teens who are deprived of the physical education intervention of caring and savvy teachers. I was overweight as a preadolescent. I grew up in the seacoast town of Hull, Massachusetts. Hull's main employer was Paragon Amusement Park, which was located on Nantasket Beach. The park, along with the beach, catered to thousands of day-trippers from the Boston area in the summer and was a bustling place. However, come fall and winter, many local residents were unemployed or trekked into Boston for low-paying jobs.

Hull was not a wealthy suburb coveted by educated and successful professionals. It was a blue-collar town with a great deal of poverty and schools that left much to be desired. In fact, there was no high school in Hull. Come grade nine, students were bused to nearby Hingham High School. Hingham was, and is, a wealthy suburban town inhabited by many college-educated families who valued education and encouraged their children to value academic success and seek a college education.

In a sense, there were two worlds at Hingham High. There were the Hull students, who were often poor academic students, had high absentee and truancy rates, brought brown-bag lunches because they couldn't afford to eat a hot lunch in the cafeteria, and had few hopes and dreams for the future except to enter the armed forces. Meanwhile, the majority of students from Hingham were successful students, didn't act out by being truant or fighting, dressed in preppy clothes, and had hopes and dreams for the future, a future that included college, not entry into the armed forces or work, as was the case for many Hull students.

Still, the "haves" of Hingham and the "have-nots" of Hull did mesh around the athletic teams at the schools. Many Hull students like me found their place through participation in sports and struck up close relationships with coaches who provided mentoring that encouraged teens like me to have hopes and dreams and even consider the possibility that college was possible. More on that later.

I grew up in a family of four children; I was the oldest. We were poor. My dad worked two jobs and our family was barely able to make ends meet, as my mom said. Our daily diet was mainly fried foods such as eggs, fish cakes, chicken, hamburgers, and Spam; macaroni and cheese; lots of potatoes and pasta; hot dogs and beans; canned soup; canned fruits; cereal with sugar; drinks with sugar; ice cream; and so on. Fresh fruits and vegetables were seldom seen. The bag lunches we took to school were usually cheese, peanut butter and jelly, or even bean sandwiches—foods that would fill us up. My daily diet was not much different from that of my peers.

We were poor kids from a poor neighborhood, a neighborhood in which many adults were overweight, abused alcohol and tobacco, and were ill with diabetes, heart conditions, and cancers, particularly the men, many of whom died far too early in life. My mother and father were very bright and caring people but this was the life they knew. Survival was the name of the game and food was part of that survival. We ate what was cheap and available. The dining experience was not one to enjoy or to help improve one's health and energy; it was meant to keep one filled and going, doing.

By seventh grade I was overweight, inactive, and not doing well in school. Our school had not had regular gym class. Recess meant every guy and gal for himself or herself, with daily fights and bullying. No adult supervision, no games, no sports equipment. Just another place where the main goal was to survive. It was kind of like a prison yard where the inmates are turned loose with no need for an intervention program or plan. It was a "let them work out their hostilities so we won't have to deal with it" approach.

In the schoolyard I was called many of the same names [as] other overweight kids. I can still remember them: "Fibkins is a loser, a slob, funny pregnant tub." No faculty member or administrator intervened or seemed to care that I was taking a lot of hits from the school bullies. I knew instinctively that I was on my own, but I didn't know I was headed for serious health problems, following in the path of many men in my neighborhood who abused food and alcohol to quiet the demons that come with working too hard and for too many hours to stay above the poverty line. They were paying the bills, making ends meet, but with no money left over except for taking a summer day trip to a nearby beach for a treat of fried clams and fries, buying a case of beer and a pack of Camel cigarettes on a Friday night, and falling asleep while listening to a Red Sox game or a Celtics basketball game. They were exhausted from a work week in which there was little or no play time or exercise.

The only kids I heard talk about exercise at school were the so-called rich kids. Many of them rode new bikes, knew how to play sports, and talked of play time or outings with their parents. They brought their lunches in colorful lunchboxes, not bags, lunchboxes that were beautifully arranged with fresh fruit, wrapped sandwiches, and insulated drink containers with milk and juice. I envied them their lifestyle.

And I was also angry, like many poor teens today, that these kids had it better than I did. I was eating baked bean sandwiches that soaked through my brown bag by lunchtime and wearing Army clothes left over from World War II, while they were eating chicken salad sandwiches with fresh lettuce and tomato and wearing preppy clothes and shoes. And I was angry that many of those kids were thin, not being exposed to the name-calling that goes with being overweight.

However, I can also relate personally and professionally to how teenagers can be helped when a caring, savvy physical education teacher or coach comes into their lives, takes notice of their lack of fitness and well being, and intervenes to direct them toward a healthier lifestyle. I was helped by three educators who not only taught me to be healthier but also were career models for me. I now work out ninety minutes each day and follow a low-fat diet. I walk outdoors, bike frequently, and use the elliptical machine and weights at a health club, a pattern that began to emerge when physical education teachers Bill Carmichael and Ervin Fieger and coach Ward Donner entered my life. That story explains why I am a champion of rigorous physical activity in our schools.

Recreation director and coach Bill Carmichael came into my life in ninth grade. Bill was hired to start a recreation program for the youth in town at the new junior high gym. Bill was a veteran who went to college after serving in the Army. He played college football and received a degree in physical education and recreation. But Bill was no ordinary beginning teacher. He was married with three children, very mature, and had a day job at a residential home for teens. He exuded confidence, was a guy who knew his way around the world, and had a welcoming, supportive demeanor. Word quickly got around the town that Bill was offering something special at the gym.

In a matter of months the gym was crowded every night from Monday through Friday. As one of my friends said, "Forget the homework; let's go have fun." Clearly the majority of teens at the evening gym, like me, were not on the road to academic success. Many of us skipped school at Hingham High at least once a week and headed into Boston to spend the day hanging out in movie theaters and even bars. We were using and abusing alcohol and tobacco bought for us by older classmates.

School was a place one had to go, but many teens in our neighborhood lacked academic and career goals and role models. Many Hull students dropped out before graduation. The ones who made it to graduation were often urged to join the armed forces by the school's guidance counselor. It seemed the only Hull teens who made it to college went on because of the support of their athletic abilities.

So the arrival of Bill Carmichael in the lives of Hull teens was sort of a miracle. Bill quickly organized a three-hour nightly regimen. We learned how to run, play basketball and baseball, lift weights, and do gymnastics; competed athletically with other recreation programs; and took regular field trips to swim at a local college and watch college and professional sports. Bill also made an effort to single out each of the gym participants for praise and to encourage them to value education and have hopes and dreams for the future.

He made it a point to encourage healthy eating and drinking and to avoid alcohol and tobacco. Part of that ritual included weighing ourselves on a regular basis, talking in my case about how to lose weight, and learning how to eat better even though money was tight at home. During my three-year stint with Bill, I lost forty-five pounds! I still remember him saying to me, "Bill, you could be a good basketball player, but we need to work on slimming you down so you can move faster."

It wasn't me doing it on my own; it was us working together on my weight loss and diet. Bill also wanted to know all about our family lives, the good and the bad, our schooling, and what mischief we were creating for ourselves. We trusted him and could talk about personal things we usually kept to ourselves.

Bill also let us know about himself. He talked about his own late start going to college after his armed service stint, marrying early, and having three kids at home and his day job with kids with disabilities. He invited us to his home for special occasions and we saw firsthand what life was like in a home where people were not living paycheck to paycheck. Many of us gym rats, as we were called, found in Bill an adult mentor whom we wanted to be like. It was no surprise that many of us found our way into teaching and coaching because of his quiet and steady influence.

I learned the important lesson that one skilled adult can indeed intervene to help many teens by being present in their lives and teaching them that a healthier and more successful lifestyle is possible, within their reach. Bill was a gift for me and my peers at a time in our lives when we needed a positive role model who stressed that we had worth and value and that we could contribute to the world in our own unique way. We had something to offer others.

Bill, in a real sense, helped raise me and taught me about the adult world along with my mother and father, who welcomed Bill's presence in my life. They saw the difference he made in me, a difference they alone could not make. We were all in it together.

Ervin Fieger entered my life in grade ten. Fieger was the boys' physical education teacher and basketball coach. He, like Bill, was a veteran and had entered the teaching profession in his early thirties. He was the model of a fit, healthy, energetic physical education teacher and coach. He was always on time, prepared, and expecting students to be involved. I never saw him just "throw out the ball" and sit on the sidelines until the period ended. He was also a caring and temperate educator who was interested in having his students enjoy the gym and the activities it offered.

Coach Fieger was the same way coaching basketball. He was interested in developing winning teams, which he did, but he also wanted his players to learn about teamwork and sharing the ball with others, to be patient and accepting when games went badly, and to show respect for the other team. He was into personal and health development for his players, stressing the need to be on time, rested, eating a healthy diet (which he described for us), and allowing no put-downs of players on our team or the opposing team.

He said, "Avoid reading your press clippings. Things can change quickly for would-be stars." He also had a calming "I know we can succeed here" approach in close contests. He wasn't a yeller, a screamer, or the type to respond with anger when the referees seemed to make bad calls.

In the fall of tenth grade Bill Carmichael urged me to go out for the junior varsity basketball team. He felt that I was ready to earn a spot. In fact, Fieger approached me in the fall and asked me to try out. He, too, suggested that I try to lose some weight as it might help me earn a spot on the team. I did make the team but at first felt overwhelmed by the other players, all of whom came from Hingham and had played together through the early grades and junior high. Fieger seemed to understand my feeling of being out of the loop and constantly tried to work me into the team, stressing that my height could help the team's defense and offensive rebounding.

With Fieger's intervention, along with Bill Carmichael's guidance, I continued to lose weight and made the starting five in my junior and senior years. I was not a star player. I had no future as a college player. But I had found another home and mentor/parent figure in Ervin Fieger and the basketball team. That home helped me establish strong personal ties with Hingham kids, and I became more involved in school social activities and became a much-improved academic student after failing most of my classes in ninth grade.

Finding a home in school and an adult mentor who can play some of the roles missing in one's home life can serve to promote pride in oneself, lead to improvement in health and academics, and assist in the search for a healthy and rewarding lifestyle and one's place in the world.

Coach Ward Donner also was a big influence in my continued weight loss and my path to becoming fit. Donner was the head coach of football, basketball, and baseball at Thayer Academy in Braintree, Massachusetts. While most of my Hull peers joined the Army, Air Force, or Marines after graduation, I decided to continue my studies at Thayer, a nearby day college preparatory school. This was my next step in discovering I could fit in with achieving students from so-called good families who lived in the wealthy suburbs of Boston. At Thayer I found other athletes from poor areas who were postgrad students trying to use athletics as a stepping-stone to college scholarships.

But more importantly, I found in Ward Donner a real teacher. Donner was the school's head administrator and disciplinarian as well as a coach. He had attended an Ivy League college, where he excelled in sports and academics. He had come to Thayer as a young teacher and coach and stayed on to establish himself as a beloved educator, mentor, and coach for the many Thayer grads who moved on to college and professional successes.

He was also a gentleman's gentleman, dressed in Brooks Brothers shirts, jacket, pants, socks, and shoes, with a different striped tie every day. He was Mr. Ivy League. He had a quiet but caring demeanor, never saying too much while coaching and disciplining students but always a good listener, available and willing to offer both praise and tempered criticism in sports and academics and expecting the best from his students and players.

Ward Donner, like Bill Carmichael and Ervin Fieger, helped me to fit in. I played basketball and baseball for him. He stressed physical and mental preparation, urging a daily running and workout regimen. Donner's teams played in a college-prep league that took us to private day and boarding schools all over New England. It was a real eye-opener for a once-overweight teen from Hull who had been on the road to perhaps dropping out of high school and at risk for a shortened lifespan like the men in his neighborhood. Now I was on the road to visiting and competing against, as Donner said, the best-prepared and brightest students in the world. I was fit, in the club, as the saying goes, and a contender.

It's no wonder that during my Thayer experience I decided that I wanted a career as an educator, to be like Carmichael, Fieger, and Donner. I wanted to do for others what they had done for me. I had found my niche. So I know something about the need for physical education teachers and coaches to intervene with overweight and obese students because I am a successful case study and a disciple of what intervention can bring.

There are two kinds of recognition in our secondary schools. One is the formal reward given for outstanding academic, arts, athletic, and citizenship performance. But there is another, often not spoken about—recognition for acts of kindness and courage in assisting students in need. These are what might be called "grapevine" awards, affirmations that trickle through the informal grapevine of school conversations announcing good deeds performed by members of the school community. An example might be a teacher who came to the rescue of a student overdosing on drugs at a school dance by calling for medical help before it was too late.

Those grapevine awards often go to teachers such as the angel teachers mentioned above and also to peers such as Mike Weber, who helped Renee connect with drama teacher Gloria Withers, or to school administrators like the middle school principal who encouraged Adam to seek out Dave Gillespie if he found it rough going at the high school.

There were also support people who made themselves available as back-ups and advisors to the helping process: Bill Borden, school social worker; counselors Ms. Mulvey, Frank Testa, Marge Holovak, and Jack Ryan; school nurse Sandi Ryan; student assistance counselor Martha Dixon; teacher Tom Murray; and administrators Sal Alvarez and Frank Middleton.

Each added their own unique skills to the process, listening and paying attention when attention was needed. It takes many members of the school community to say "yes" to another's distress and make time to hear the story. These angels don't hide behind the selfish reasoning that says "this is not my job, not my role, not my responsibility, not something I can handle."

Angel teachers don't know all the rules or the rights and wrongs of helping others but one thing they do know is that help is necessary and they are being called upon to help. They are chosen for service and they do not hide from this request. At times answering these calls can raise many questions, concerns, fears, and anxiety.

Often, angel teachers arrive at this special place having survived a troubled, even abusive, childhood themselves. They know the territory of a fragmented family life, a child's fright, the absence of safety and protection, having no one to answer when they cry for help. They know the feeling of determination that one has to muster to be able to survive, save oneself, maintain hope, and find a way out of the family's misery. They remember being in a family when their lives took a turn for the worse and the bottom fell out. And they remember knowing things they really didn't want to know about each other.

Many angel teachers found their way out and a road to a happier life by being helped by teachers. As a result angel teachers understand the same kinds of troubles that can visit their students in some form. They understand the randomness of their students' life experiences. Their students will all get hit by life's blows in some form, but for some the blows will be more staggering. Some will have a near miss while others will experience a disaster.

It all comes down to belief—believing one can make a positive difference by entering the other's world and bringing some calm, clarity, and hope to the other's life. Think of yourself, whether you are a teacher, administrator, student, support staff, or parent, as someone who holds a candle that can light the path to help teens heading towards trouble or wanting to get out of trouble. Every light along the path matters. If one is extinguished, it leaves another layer of darkness and makes the path longer, more treacherous, and allows failure to become an option.

Many people are needed for the helping process to work. We should never underestimate what a few kind words can do to open a new door for those in trouble. We know more about helping than we admit simply because we ourselves have lived a life and experienced tough times. Angel teachers understand this and use their own life experience as a guide.

Bill Keller, a writer for and former executive editor of the *New York Times*, uses a quote from the poet Shelley to put the work of angel teachers into perspective. Shelley wrote, "A man, to be greatly good, must imagine intensely and comprehensively; he must put himself in the place of another and of many others; the pains and pleasures of his species must become his own."[2]

NOTES

1. William L. Fibkins, *Teen Obesity: How Schools Can Be the Number One Solution to the Problem* (Lanham, MD: Rowman & Littlefield, 2006), 150–57.

2. Bill Keller, "I Yield My Time to the Gentleman from Stratford-Upon-Avon," *The New York Times Magazine*, August 14, 2011, 11, 12.

Chapter Three

The Presence of Angel Teachers Might Save the Lives of Desperate Teenagers

Angel teachers cannot be everywhere. There are simply not enough of them to go around. Some teens in trouble will be missed. They are often students who are highly successful, seemingly absent of troubles and on the road to a highly successful life. Many do have problems but they are able to hide them from view. Hide them, that is, until their problems become unmanageable. Reaching out for help has never been their style. As a result some kids don't get the help they need and death arrives too early, lives lost that might have been saved. Such was the case for Scott Croteau, Taylor Hooton, and J. Daniel Scruggs.

For very talented students like Scott Croteau, the approach is being strong, showing no cracks in their demeanor, at least cracks not easily seen by family members, peers, teachers, counselors, or school administrators. They're the kids who are not supposed to have problems and when problems do occur, these kids don't know where to turn. It as if they have no license to be human and falter, even fail. They are left searching for a way out and that way out is often a self-inflicted bullet to the head, a drug overdose, slashing their wrists, or rising in the middle of the night to stand in front of a racing train or car.

One day they are alive and are leaders in their schools. They next day they are dead. The news is surreal, met with comments like "it can't be true," "impossible," "there must be some mistake." Its news that leaves family members, peers, teachers, and neighbors wondering how they missed the signs of this student's great distress and what they might have done to intervene. The answer to their concerns is often overly simple. They were looking in the wrong place, looking at what the teen accomplished in school, on the playing field, and what he or she added to the school community with that never-ending track record of success.

They missed the little telltale signs that might have signaled a teen at risk. Their binoculars weren't programmed to notice small behavioral changes. They were blinded by the glare of success we focus on some students, the cult in which everyone likes a winner and avoids seeing cracks in their champions.

Such was the case of Scott Croteau,[1] seventeen, a gifted student who is viewed as the *perfect* teen and anointed as the standard bearer of his school. Scott masks his personal problems, except for a few clues that no one seems to notice and is so tormented that he commits suicide, an act no one in the community can understand.

There was, it seems, no angel teacher to come to his aid. He died alone. This story provides a wake-up call for the need to have more angel teachers in our schools, teachers who don't look the other way when they observe behavior changes that spell trouble and are ready and able to intervene before it's too late. It's needed for all students but particularly for our best and brightest teens whom the school community has elevated to stardom and who seem so perfect. Too perfect.

Scott Croteau, seventeen, was a senior and perhaps the most popular student at Lewiston High, a pride of the heavily French-Canadian community, co-captain of the football team, and a straight-A student who had a stack of more than fifteen recruiting letters on his desk at home from colleges like Harvard and Princeton and Holy Cross. Yet he committed suicide. The state medical examiner would determine that the "manner of death was by self-inflicted gunshot wound and hanging." It was deemed a "double suicide." Many Lewiston students and townspeople, including Croteau's father, couldn't and wouldn't believe that Scott had committed suicide. There was no note, and no clues. He always seemed too good to be true, and so driven, so focused on his goals. Scott's parents were divorced and had a history involving many confrontations.

Clearly, Scott Croteau carried a heavy burden given the prolonged turmoil in his home life. It appears he tried to save himself and find his way out of a troubled life by excelling in academics, athletics, and being the all-around good kid—liked by everyone, popular, no enemies, well-mannered, humble, modest to a fault, nice, never complaining, straight arrow. He was a child of troubled parents who used his school success to show others that his life was all right in spite of his home situation.

He was nonconfrontational, never got into fights, He didn't get into situations that were confrontational and might require him to fight back. In his last month he noticed his mother watching him in football practice from a distance but made no effort to speak to her. It seemed he never lashed out at either of his parents for disrupting his life for so many years. He wasn't a fighter and he avoided confrontation. He was the good child.

One can theorize that Scott carried a lot of anger that he kept buried. The clues were there but covered over by his niceness. Some of his peers said it seemed no one knew what Scott's feelings were, that he seemed to hide behind his striving for perfection. He always seemed too good to be true to them, so driven, so focused on his goals. In retrospect, they felt he was depressed.

It appears there were no designated helpers or angel teachers to help him understand and resolve his demons. Maybe if he had been the kind of troubled teen who acted out, did drugs, started fights, and failed subjects, the designated helpers in the school would have acted. But they were probably blindsided by Scott's niceness and success.

Teens who act out and make mischief have a better chance of getting intervention because they create problems for the school community. Nice kids like Scott don't really get noticed except for their resumes. They don't make trouble, only positive headlines in the local newspapers and other media. They are held to a higher standard, sometimes—as in Scott's case—too high. Others—students, teachers, administrators, and community members—expect and demand a lot from them.

As some peers admitted, they didn't really know what Scott's feelings really were. He seemed to hide behind his striving for perfection. Being too bright, too successful in school and too nice may appear to be positive behaviors and character traits, but they may also be warning signs and raise a red flag for designated helpers.

Scott's sad and untimely death documents the need to have angel teachers in the school who can look more closely at students, even the best and brightest like Scott, and begin a helping conversation that goes like this:

"Hi, Scott. How are you doing with all this college pressure? I've heard you received over fifty recruiting letters from schools such as Harvard and Holy Cross. How about lunch tomorrow? I'd like to hear how you're holding up with all this stuff—football, advanced placement classes, and so forth. There's a new pizza place on High Street. I see your lunch is fifth period, same as mine. I'll meet you in the faculty parking lot at lunch time."

A few simple words of interest and concern can save lives. It might have saved Scott Croteau's.

There were a few staff members at the high school who sensed Scott was in deep trouble, maybe a teacher, coach, administrator or counselor, people who felt they weren't experienced enough in mental health issues to act. It is not uncommon for professionals lacking mental health credentials to think they are unqualified to act, and thus they deny what they observe. They simply don't believe they have the skills to act or have the belief that they should.

This is not a case of teachers who choose to look the other way when they observe a teen in trouble. Rather, these are teachers who care deeply about kids like Scott but feel they are on shaky ground about intervening or calling for help. Someone in Scott's school, maybe more than one someone, probably regrets to this day that they failed to make the call for help. They distrusted their own feelings.

Given the segregated and controlled process of who is authorized to give help, this is an all-too-common practice. It is not the fault of the caring teacher but rather an example of how the helping process often works in our secondary schools to the detriment of needy students. It's one more reason that we need savvy angel teachers on board who are equipped and committed to sounding the alarm. We need professionals who can deliver when lives are on the line and time is running out, not wait or leave it to the designated helpers to sound the alarm, an alarm, it appears, that was never rung for Scott.

The story of Taylor Hooton is different but had the same tragic ending. Close friends, teachers, coaches, and parents are important resources in steering students who are headed for trouble into intervention. They are on the front lines and quickly see students headed toward the margins. They can offer initial intervention that can, in some cases, save the lives of students. However, many students, educators, and parents do not see themselves as their brothers' keepers. They may see dramatic changes in a student's demeanor, behavior, and emotional/physical well being but hesitate to intervene or share their concern with the school's intervention specialist because they fail to trust their own observations and insights that something is going wrong.

Billy Ajello is one of those caring high school students. Ajello, a catcher on the Plano, Texas, West Senior High School baseball team, had many concerns about Taylor Hooton, his best friend and pitcher on the team. And his concerns were well-placed. On July 15, 2003, a month past his seventeenth birthday, Taylor killed himself. The authorities ruled the death a suicide by hanging.

As writer Jere Longman reports,[2] Taylor's parents and a doctor familiar with the case said that they believe that Taylor's death was related to depression that he felt upon discontinuing the use of anabolic steroids. A sense of euphoria and aggression can be replaced by lethargy, loss of self-confidence, melancholy, and hopelessness when a person stops using performance-enhancing drugs.

Dr. Larry W. Gibson, medical director of the Cooper Aerobics Center, a leading preventive medicine clinic in Dallas, said, "It's a pretty strong case that Taylor was withdrawing from steroids and his suicide was directly related to it. This is a kid who was well-liked and had a lot of friends, no serious emotional problems. He had a bright future."

Looking back, there were many signals that Taylor was heading for trouble. He was described as a young man who smiled often, was popular with girls, and had many friends from different backgrounds. He was polite and respectful. Blake Blydston, the baseball coach at Plano West, said, "He always came to the field in good spirits. When he spoke, it was, 'Thank you; no, sir; yes, sir.' And as Ajello said, "You counted on the kid to throw strikes."

After Taylor's death his parents said they had learned from his psychiatrist that he had low self-esteem and that to feel as if he measured up, he had to make himself look bigger, drive a big pickup truck. A junior high coach had also suggested to Taylor that he get bigger, his father, Don Hooton, said. During chemistry class in the fall of 2002 Taylor mentioned to Ajello that he might begin using steroids. Ajello asked why and Taylor replied, "I'm not doing it for baseball. I'm doing it for myself."

There was a dark side to Taylor. Late in the winter and into the spring Don and Gwen Hooton noticed changes in Taylor's physique and behavior. Taylor, who was six feet one and a half inches tall, grew to 205 pounds from about 175 pounds. Initially, his parents did not suspect steroid use. Don

Hooton said he felt proud that his son seemed to be working hard in the weight room. Taylor began to develop acne on his back and exhibit signs of aggressiveness and irritability. He flew into rages and then became tearfully apologetic. He took several hundred dollars from his parents' bank account without permission. He would pound the floor with his fists in anger. Once, he punched a wall and injured a knuckle on his pitching hand. During a rage in April he told his mother, "I'll just take a knife and end it now."

His parents sent him to a psychiatrist. Taylor told the doctor that he had been injecting himself with the steroid Deca 300 and taking oral Anadrol. By May 19, Taylor said he had stopped using the drugs. But on a trip to England in July, Taylor stole a digital camera and laptop computer, his father said. When his family returned on July 14, his parents, brother, and sister confronted Taylor and told him that his behavior had become unacceptable. He was grounded.

The next morning, Taylor asked his mother to lift the punishment, but she said no. He went upstairs and, using belts to fashion a noose, hung himself from the door to his bedroom, Don Hooton said. Later, when police inspected Taylor's room, vials of steroids along with syringes and needles were found. An autopsy revealed the presence of metabolized steroids, 19-norandrosterone and 19-noretiocholanolone, in Taylor's system, a report from the Collins County Medical Examiner said.

Billy Ajello said he had warned Taylor about the health risks of steroids but that Taylor "kind of blew it off." Apparently none of Taylor's friends alerted an adult. Did Taylor's brother, Donald, intervene to help Taylor once he reported his use of steroids? Clearly Taylor's parents saw the danger and sent him to a psychiatrist. Clearly his close friend Billy Ajello tried to warn him. But it appears no adults or students in the school sensed that Taylor was becoming increasingly troubled.

What is needed at the Plano West Senior High Schools of the world are many open doors for intervention, the kinds of open doors that might have saved Taylor's life—open doors through which Taylor himself, his parents, Billy Ajello, concerned coaches, and teachers and peers could walk to get help and share their concerns.

That would entail educating close friends, students, teachers, coaches, and parents that their observations are important and matter. It also means having in place an intervention system that can quickly respond and work closely with a psychiatrist and develop a shared intervention plan that provides a safety net for the Taylors of this world. The issue isn't about blaming school officials, staff, students, or parents for not acting. There is always blame and sometimes denial involved in such cases.

Billy Ajello said, "They want to pretend it didn't happen. The administration will probably tell you otherwise but from a student's perspective it's done, it's over with." Phil Saviano, the principal of Plano West, said Taylor Hooton's death was his first encounter with steroids. Mike Hughes, the athletic director and football coach, said, "I have been in the district twenty-one years and I have not known of a kid that was on steroids."

Here is another story, different but with the same ending. As reporter Marc Santora tells the story,[3] well before J. Daniel Scruggs, twelve, hanged himself in his closet using one of his neckties, it was clear he was having some kind of trouble. He had failed to show up or was late for school seventy-four of the past seventy-eight days, complaining that he was being relentlessly bullied. He had taken to defecating and urinating in his pants, rarely washed, and had very bad breath and body odor.

Hours after he died in January 2002, the police entered his home in Meriden, Connecticut, and described the home as a total mess where clothes, trash, and debris littered every room. Connecticut state prosecutors criminally charged the boy's mother, Judith Scruggs, in connection with his suicide, claiming her failure to get her son proper counseling put him at undue risk.

During the court proceedings, Melissa Smith, a classmate of Daniel's, testified that he was subjected to relentless bullying at school because he was considered different. "People would spit on his chairs. Sometimes he would ignore it, sometimes he looked like he was going to cry, and sometimes he yelled and got into trouble for it." She described times when Daniel was yelled at, punched, kicked, and even thrown off the bleachers in the gym without teachers ever coming to his aid.

His death prompted the creation of an advocacy group for parents and children who are bullied and the passage of a state law requiring that schools develop a system to report bullying. The case drew national attention because an investigation by the state's child advocate and chief state attorney immediately after the suicide found the boy's complaints about bullying had gone unanswered. Mrs. Scruggs, a single parent, was found guilty of putting her child at risk and of cruelty to a person.

There is a lot of blame to go around but it seems the breakdown of help for Daniel is systemic. There appears to have been no intervention system established in the school that could come to the aid of a very troubled boy when his shouts for help must certainly have been heard by educators, peers, and parents. Was anyone except perhaps classmate Melissa Smith looking closer?

Keep in mind that it is the closer look that gets at the problem that no one else at home or at school is noticing. Clearly, a teacher, secretary, school nurse, assistant principal, bus driver, hallway monitor, gym teacher, caring peer, or a concerned neighbor must have noticed Daniel's increased fear and struggle. Kid shouldn't have to go to school to be beaten up or return to a home where they are not cared for. There appear to have been no open doors for Daniel to get help and support and no open doors for concerned peers like Melissa Smith, support staff, educators, or parents to share their concern and receive needed advice on how to intervene to help Daniel.

In the end, it appears that Daniel was on his own and lacking any hope that things might change. Enough was enough for this twelve-year-old. Hanging was his way out of the ongoing struggle. What a pity! Things might have been different if he had been involved in a school community that was ready and set to respond to his many needs. Daniel lacked a personal adult advocate in his school who could have easily observed the troubling data that was emerging and acted to intervene. Daniel's deteriorating march toward the margins of school and community life could have easily been tracked through his tardiness, truancy, lack of physical and emotional well being, and being the target of relentless bullying.

It appears that teachers failed to convey a sense of caring for Daniel and engage his family as partners in his education. And it appears that the school failed to successfully interact with hard-to-reach parents with activities such as home visits, Saturday meetings, and meetings outside of regular business hours. Mrs. Scruggs was also on her own without help and support. Where was the connection between he school and agencies in the community to help coordinate the delivery of physical and mental health and social services for Daniel and his mom? Where was Daniel's angel teacher?

NOTES

1. Ira Berkow, "An Athlete Is Dead at 17 and No One Can Say Why," *New York Times*, October 1, 1995, C 1.

2. Jere Longman, "An Athlete's Dangerous Experiment," *New York Times*, November 26, 2003, pp1, 4 (D).

3. Marc Santora, "Case Tries to Link a Mother to Her Boy's Suicide," *New York Times*, September 27, 2003, page 1, 6 (B).

Chapter Four

The Skills, Concerns, Issues, and Ongoing Training Needs of Angel Teachers

Many of the problems that teens face endure generation after generation—alcohol, drug, and tobacco addiction; sexual, physical, or emotional abuse; school failure; family dysfunction and violence; illness or death of loved ones; divorce; eating disorders. These are the *usual suspects* awaiting naïve, unskilled, and trusting teens and they are ever-present in the school community. No matter how familiar these problems are to the school community, each time they occur, they can have a devastating impact on students experiencing these problems.

Yet sometimes the labels and words describing teen problems, such as student suicides, can sound overly clinical and mask the personal trauma affecting students left behind to figure out what went wrong and worry if the same thing could happen to them.

I say "overly clinical" in the sense that data such as the percentage of students committing suicide at the national level and the warning signs exhibited by potential suicide victims often make the news following a student's suicide rather than the real stories and intimate details involved in such a hopeless act. Teens are shielded because adults in the community feel they are not up to dealing with the pain in the stories. Protection of teens can prevent them from acquiring necessary skills. We do them no favors in our efforts to save them from the tragedies of life that can visit all of us. There are important lessons to be learned from loss and crisis.

It is pain they are entitled to hear about as they seek to understand life. Life is not all flowers and sunshine. People do get waylaid by life's problems. It's a dark side that teens are entitled to hear about but are often denied. Denied, that is, until a helper such as an angel teacher enters the teen's world and hears through sobs and anger the unclinical, real story. Angel teachers can use this terrible event as a teaching moment so that students understand that it's better to get help before the bottom falls out of their lives.

Many teens in our society simply don't know how to behave in the face of death, how to think and feel and talk about death. They don't have a parent like the one James Agee describes in *A Death in the Family*,[1] who consoles her children after the death of their father. Here is what she says, offering comfort and hope in a few well-chosen words:

> "And you understand that, when God takes you away to heaven, you can never come back?"
>
> "Never come back?" Catherine asked.
>
> She stroked Catherine's hair away from her face. "No, Catherine, not ever, in any way we can see and talk to. Daddy's soul will always be thinking of us, just as we will always think of him, but we will never see him again, after today." Catherine looked at her very intently; her face began to redden. "You must learn to believe that and know it, darling Catherine. It is so."
>
> She seemed to be about to cry; she swallowed. Catherine seemed to accept it as true.
>
> "We'll always remember him," she told both of them. "Always. And he'll be thinking of us. Every day. He's waiting for us in heaven. And someday, if we're good, when God comes for us, He'll take us to heaven too and we'll see Daddy there, and all be together again, forever and ever."
>
> "Amen," Rufus almost said, then realized that this was not a prayer.
>
> "But when we see Daddy today, children, his soul won't be there. It'll just be Daddy's body. Very much as you've always seen him. But because his soul has been taken away, he will be lying down, and he will lie very still. It will be just as if he were asleep and you didn't want to wake him. Quieter."

The mother in Agee's *A Death in the Family* tries to prepare her children for the father's funeral. She can't take away the shock of death but she can tell her children what to expect. They are lucky.

There are problems that often break out with little warning, such as a student death in a car accident, a student becoming the victim of a life-threatening sexually transmitted disease, or a poor economy that spawns unemployment for many workers and results in the breakdown of family life, addictions, or abuse. These are problems that can bring lingering distress for students, who ask, "Why me? What went wrong? Why my family?" The bottom can fall out unexpectedly for teenagers. No one sees it coming but when it arrives it is devastating to the life that was so familiar, even yesterday.

The work of angel teachers to improve their helping skills is a work in progress, a path in which they try to avoid becoming too comfortable, all-knowing, with teenage problems. For teens experiencing personal problems for the first time, there is often little or no comfort. It can be a painful, sometimes nightmarish experience. They often find themselves alone trying to figure things out, alone either by choice or because no one else seems to care. They need a caring adult to break down their isolation, a skilled advocate who knows how they feel.

Here are some of the skill areas angel teachers try to master in order to convince troubled teens that they understand the problem and to get them on board the helping process:

- Being a good, nonjudgmental listener
- Creating a trusting, caring, and supportive environment
- Being loyal and holding the confidence of students unless a serious health or emotional issue emerges
- Knowing how to hold successful one-on-one and group conversations with students
- Knowing when, where, and how to make good referrals when serious trouble emerges
- Being aware of the characteristics of the students and problems they tend to avoid as angel teachers. We all come into teaching with our own biases and unease with certain students. They make us feel anxious and intimidated. Some problems that students experience have the same effect. We want to avoid these students and problems. This is only natural. Instead of running, successful angel teachers work to learn ways to overcome these barriers and accept their resistance as a necessary glitch to overcome in the helping process.

- Being aware of the kinds of students and problems they are attracted to and tend to spend too much time with, at the expense of other students in need. These students and problems are in line with our comfort zones; no fear, anxiety, or unease here. Successful angel teachers need to be aware of their comfort zones and not let them control which students they like to help and which problems they like to deal with.
- Knowing how to advocate for students with colleagues, administrators, parents, and community law, health, mental health, and social service agencies.
- Knowing how to maintain close and intimate contact with students without crossing professional boundaries. Students need to know teachers' limits and that they have personal lives. Teachers cannot be their friends, parents, or 24/7 confidantes.
- Creating sources of support both within the school community and in their personal lives. Angel teachers need resources of their own that they can turn to for support and honest feedback. These are their *go-to* people when the path to help is complicated and unclear.
- Providing a classroom meeting area where they meet one-on-one or in small groups with students that is an attractive setting that encourages students to feel comfortable, safe, wanted, and open to sharing.

In addition to their own skill development, angel teachers need to remind themselves what's in it for them in their helping role. Sometimes in the battle to help troubled teens, they get worn down and need to be reminded why they are in this important work.

Here are some reasons that angel teachers say they do what they do:

- They want to be a teacher who is skilled and committed to intervention as well as a subject teacher, instead of one who is simply a subject teacher uninvolved in the personal side of students' lives.
- In many cases angel teachers are involved in helping troubled teens because they themselves were helped as teens by caring teachers, coaches, ministers, recreation supervisors, police personnel, etc.
- The skills used to help them are the same skills they are using to help troubled teens. They know what works because it worked for them. They are simply carrying on the mission taught them by caring adults.

- By trying to help teens whom they find difficult, even intimidating, they are able to improve their subject matter skills and increasingly help all their students, not just the ones they feel comfortable with. Their goal is to move closer to these students and reduce the isolation between them. Teens know when teachers choose to avoid them.
- By trying to help teens with problems that the angel teachers find threatening, they are able to improve their subject matter teaching and increasingly involve all their students, not just ones with problems that fit well into their comfort zones. Again, their goal is to move closer to students who have problems that threaten them, not isolate them. Teens know when teachers choose to avoid their problems.
- Teaming with like-minded natural allies, such as counselors skilled in intervention, creates a new layer of help for troubled teens. This new layer of help allows and encourages teens to walk through many open doors for help, not limiting them to visits to the offices of sometimes overburdened counselors. Help is available in many areas and each is worthwhile and necessary.
- Angel teachers have pride. They are not uninvolved teachers whose response to troubled teens is to send them off to make an appointment with some distant helper, which most teens never do. Once uninvolved teachers send troubled students on their way, they are no longer involved nor do they feel a responsibility for what happens next in the helping process. In contrast, angel teachers are involved directly and take a leadership role in the helping process. They feel they are responsible for helping troubled teens get the help they need. That's their goal and their challenge.
- Angel teachers remember that one bad moment for teens can turn their entire lives upside down. It's a shame because up until now they've been so good. One bad moment can be a life sentence in high school. Angel teachers are there to make sure that one bad moment doesn't result in a fixed label that can taint a teen's high school career or later life.
- While the role of angel teacher is different from that of a subject matter teachers, they accept that their helping role is not for every teacher. Sometimes this acceptance is made difficult by some teachers' blatant disinterest in helping troubled teens. Angel teachers understand that their mission includes being proactive in getting colleagues on board but that effort is not always successful. Some teachers are simply not cut out for this role and need to be left to be who they are, even when *who they are* doesn't sit well with angel teachers.

- Angel teachers realize that the problems teens experience can also be very painful for the teachers themselves. Intervening and responding to teen problems have their costs and downsides. The emotional roller coaster that teens describe in their lives cannot be easily fended off. Painful stories told by vulnerable teens do and should cause angst for angel teachers.

After all, we can't tell troubled teens that "we are in this together" and then run for cover when their painful stories are revealed. Rather, angel teachers try to listen and stay the course, sending the message that they are up to the task of helping no matter how painful the problem is. But that doesn't mean they go home each night and leave their feelings at the classroom door. Helping can be a risky and costly business and those angel teachers who enter the fray need to remind themselves that there is an emotional price to be paid, a price that is worth it when teens find their way out of trouble and into their niche.

Occasionally the intervention seems to fail. Sometimes it takes a long time to resolve a problem. Angel teachers need to remind themselves that their interest in intervention starts the process and can lead to help down the road.

- Angel teachers need to believe that what they are doing is important and that they are offering something special to students, parents, colleagues, natural allies, administrators, and also to themselves. They have pushed themselves out of the traditional role of teacher and created a new brand of helper in the school—a unique achievement.

Even the most effective angel teachers have issues and concerns about their helping roles. While these issues and concerns are a normal part of the process of helping others and are shared by professionals in the mental health community, they offer a window into the anxiety helpers experience in trying to get the helping job done successfully.

Helping skills need to be shared by many members of the school community so they are ready and able to act to help kids heading toward the margins of school and community life. This sharing of skills is a unique opportunity for a team of natural allies—angel teacher, counselor, school psychologist, school nurse—to offer training for teachers interested in joining the team of angel helpers. Teachers need to talk openly about their concerns with being an angel teacher before they make the decision to come on board. As one listens to their concerns, it becomes clear that this is not an easy decision, nor should it be.

Chapter 5 will illustrate the kind of training programs that could raise the skills of angel teachers beyond their natural helping abilities and encourage more subject matter teachers to take on an angel teacher role.

NOTE

1. James Agee, *A Death in the Family* (New York: Bantam, 1957), section 3.

Chapter Five

How to Upgrade the Skills of Angel Teachers and Get More Subject Matter Teachers on Board

Angel teachers perform a great function in our secondary schools. They represent a beacon of hope and help in a system that is being crippled by budget cuts, allocation of existing help resources into quasi-administrative roles such as testing and scheduling students, and making college admission counseling *the* priority for high school counselors. Intervention to help troubled teens rests with angel teachers and a few counselors who resist being quasi-administrators or stuck in the role of counselors for college-bound students. They are natural allies attempting to deliver help and, in their efforts, creating a new layer of intervention that delivers real, tangible, visible assistance, calling into question the mountains of rhetoric about the role of the designated helpers in meeting the personal needs of pupils when in fact the demands of the school bureaucracy make it impossible for counselors to fulfill this role.

However great this effort is, it can be improved with little cost. With training the skills of angel teachers can be upgraded and more subject matter teachers can be convinced to come on board as angel teachers and begin to embrace their roles as helpers. These new recruits can expand the numbers of helpers needed to make a dent in coming to the aid of troubled teens. A two-pronged training program, consisting of upgrading the skills of angel teachers and teaching newcomers helping skills, can go a long way in ensuring a more highly skilled corps that can deliver help when needed.

One additional aspect of this two-pronged approach is that seasoned angel teachers and subject matter teachers will be involved in the training together. This approach provides a unique opportunity for angel teachers to share their experiences while at the same time sharpening their own skills. This process also affirms that the important helping role of angel teachers is not just for students. This kind of training establishes them as facilitators and models in helping colleagues take on the dual role of helper and subject matter teacher.

First, some background. The personal needs of teens are not going away. Joseph Sanacore,[1] a special education professor at Long Island University, suggests that educators need to work hard to meet the academic and personal needs of students. Compounding these challenges are social issues that affect children: high divorce rates, a rise in homes with two working parents, growing unemployment, and single parents who often have to work two jobs just to get by. This has resulted in home situations in which children don't have a consistently available adult they can talk to about their daily stresses. Many teenagers try to navigate through life's challenges without an available adult to guide them.

Deborah Meier[2] reports that most children today are disconnected from any community of adults, including many teachers they encounter in school. Many young people literally finish four years of high school without knowing or being known by a single adult in the school building. Meier suggests that it is a striking fact that kids don't keep a lot of company these days with the kinds of adults, in and out of school, who they might grow up to be (or who we might wish them to grow up to be).

Meier warns that we have cut kids adrift without the support and nurturance of grownups, without the support of a community in which they might feel safe to try out various roles and listen in to the world of adults, a world they will someday join. As Meier suggests, teachers can do a better job of knowing their students well and intervening when troubles arrive at their doorsteps.

While Meier's observations are right on target, they fail to convey an important reality about the professional lives, culture, and boundaries that occupy the world of secondary school teachers. Many teachers in our secondary schools have been advised, warned, and indoctrinated that their role is teaching their subject, not helping or counseling students in need. In order to get them trained and involved in responding to the personal needs of students, that culture must change and teachers need to be released from rigid boundaries that distance them from being skilled helpers.

That means school leaders must send a clear signal that times have changed and teachers are needed in the fight to provide a safety net for students heading toward the margins of school and community life. They need to be players, not observers free to turn their heads away from students who are clearly troubled and looking to them for intervention.

Since the 1950s and the emergence of the guidance movement, counselors, followed by school psychologists and social workers, have taken over the helping role of teachers. Before these designated helpers arrived on the scene, teachers were seen as the main source of help for troubled students. They were finessed out of this helping role by the arrival of counselors who were better trained to help students and relieve classroom teachers to do what they do best, teach their students well. As a result the helping process moved farther from the informal classroom setting to professional offices to which students were "referred" for counseling appointments behind closed doors.

As a result, many classroom teachers previously committed to intervening to help troubled teens simply gave up their helping roles. Their skills weren't wanted in the large high schools that were emerging in the 1950s and 1960s. Counselor educator Harold L. Munson,[3] writing in 1971, suggests, however, that teachers have an important counseling role with students. Their role emphasized caring, trust, understanding, acceptance, and responding to personal concerns of students. Munson suggests that this should be anticipated and, when teachers feel capable and confident in dealing with these issues, they should be encouraged to do so. This is *counseling.*

However, Munson cautions that this counseling role of teachers is rapidly being taken away. He foresaw the negation of the role of the teacher as counselor and helper. Munson observes that, while many students are seeking communication with teachers, with increasing frequency teachers are urged to refer to the school counselor. As Munson states, the danger here lies in absolving the teacher of his or her rightful and expected guidance responsibility. The message, while not overtly or openly expressed, has become rather clear. Even if this is calculated only for students with problems that extend beyond the proficiency of the teacher, the expectation that the students are *treated* in the guidance office leaves the developmental needs of youth too often unattended to in the classroom.

It raises considerable doubt, fear, and guilt in the minds of teachers who respond or feel they must respond to students. Teachers have been warned repeatedly, with the advent of the guidance movement, that they are not counselors. Counseling has been increasingly a territorial claim of the school counselor, accordingly reducing the involvement of many teachers in any communication with their students that could be interpreted as counseling. It is almost as if teachers have been warned against any kind of human involvement with students. It is no wonder that many teachers have become cautious and concerned about helping students with personal issues.

Munson concludes that we need teachers who feel capable and confident in dealing with the personal matters of students, which have been for too long considered outside the realm of teachers' concern and responsibility.

Munson's comments accurately predicted the flawed helping system that exists in our secondary schools today. The historical helping role of teachers shifted to the designated helpers in the school once the guidance movement took hold in the 1950s.

Yet as counselor educator David Cook[4] suggested in 1971, while the original mandate of counseling in secondary schools was to assist all students with their developmental needs and problems, that mandate was quickly replaced with counselors given the lead role in sorting students into the right classes, colleges, and vocations.

As Cook suggests, general education counseling emerged as the main counseling concern in the schools. Many counselors who might be adequate to the task of therapeutic counseling found that the demands of the schools' organizations made it difficult, if not impossible, to carry out this kind of counseling. Cook concludes that the counselor has been seduced into functioning on behalf of the bureaucratic structure of the school. Despite a mountain of rhetoric about meeting the needs of pupils, the reality is that it was the increasing bureaucratization of our school systems that created the demand for guidance services.

The graduate level training to provide teachers with intervention skills also became a lower priority because teachers were now viewed primarily as subject matter teachers. They were told that counselors would be available to help them when they encountered students with problems, a promise that often went unfulfilled in our secondary schools, leaving teachers waiting for advice and counsel that might be a long time in coming or not coming at all.

As a result, in 2012 there are limited opportunities for students to find an available adult to be an advisor, helper, or role model. Teachers have been told for decades to stay out of the helping role and stick to their subject matter. The message has gotten through to them except for the angel teachers who dared to challenge this limited role.

Counselors have been told that their first priority is to sort students into the right classes, colleges, and vocations, even those counselors who have highly developed skills in therapeutic counseling. A vacuum of help for troubled students was created in the 1970s and in today's schools made even worse by the loss of counselors due to budget cuts and the addition of even more administrative tasks to the surviving counselors' roles, for example administering state-mandated tests.

More recently schools are also calling on guidance counselors and social workers to add to their growing list of administrative duties by being anti-bullying experts. For example, *New York Times* writer Winnie Hu[5] reports that a new state law in New Jersey, the Anti-Bullying Bill of Rights, demands that, beginning in September 2011, all public schools adopt comprehensive anti-bullying policies, increase staff training, and adhere to tight deadlines for reporting episodes. The law also requires that a school must designate an anti-bullying specialist to investigate complaints and each district must have an anti-bullying coordinator.

As a result, Hu says, in most cases schools are tapping guidance counselors and social workers as the new anti-bullying specialists, raising the question of whether they have the time or experience to look into every complaint of harassment or intimidation and write the detailed reports required. It's one more step in further bureaucratizing the guidance counselors' roles and distancing them from their counseling role for students. Teens don't seek out *specialists* and *coordinators* when they need help.

New York Times reporter Jacques Steinberg provides an open window to the gradual dismantling of the personal counseling role of high school guidance counselors and their increasing involvement as quasi-administrators. In his article "Graduates Fault Advice of Guidance Counselors,"[6] Steinberg reports that a new study has found most people who graduated from high school in the last dozen years believe that their guidance counselors provided little meaningful advice about college or careers. Many said the best advice came from teachers.

According to a study by Public Agenda, a nonprofit research organization, "most young adults who go on to college believe that the advice of their high school guidance counselor was inadequate and often impersonal and perfunctory. Most troubling and potentially significant for policy makers is that young people characterized their interactions with guidance counselors as anonymous and unhelpful." Nearly half of those interviewed said their counselors made them feel "like I was just another face in the crowd."[7]

The study notes that counselors' caseloads and responsibilities have only grown in recent years. The researchers note, "It is also important to remember that advising students on higher education choices is just one of the many things that guidance counselors do. Much of their effort is devoted to discipline issues and sorting out scheduling and other administrative mix-ups within the high school."

An interview by researchers with Jim Jump, a high school counselor who is president of the National Association of College Admission Counseling, echoed the report's findings. He expressed his concern that "so many other things are tossed on counselors' plates that actual counseling takes up a very small part of the time."

One of the important conclusions of this study is that young people typically give their teachers and mentors much better ratings than the dismal ratings assigned to guidance counselors. Solid majorities of young adults from diverse ethnic and racial backgrounds report that they had "teachers who really took an interest in them personally and encouraged them to go to college." Most say they had a teacher or coach who "really inspired them and motivated them to do their best." A student from St. Louis reported that he turned to his advanced biology teacher for help because "some teachers just care. . . . You can just tell."

This Public Agenda analysis accurately describes a system in which there is a closing of many open doors to help for teens in need of counseling, mentoring, role modeling, and good advice. It is not the fault of overwhelmed counselors, clearly not of their doing. Rather, it speaks to the current landscape in our secondary schools, in which counselors have become a wing of the administration and, as the study suggests, see much of their effort devoted to discipline issues and sorting out scheduling and other administrative mix-ups within the high school. Actual counseling takes up very little of their time.

There is no one to blame for this counselor debacle. Certainly it's not the fault of overwhelmed administrators, who need every warm body on board to keep the school running, given the daily crises of secondary school life. And it's not the fault of the counselors who are being called upon to support the administrators' efforts. Blame will not solve this problem.

This vacuum of available counseling for troubled teens has a positive element to it. Angel teachers have emerged who believe their role, a double role, includes being an academic teacher as well as a helper, and who have wisely coupled themselves with natural allies such as counselors with therapeutic counseling skills. Some of these counselors were actively searching for a venue in which to use the skills they were trained to offer, rather than spending their entire professional lives sorting students into classes, vocations, and careers. Angel teachers and their natural allies have emerged as the main resource to serve as available adults for students. We need more of them.

Mark Edmundson, a professor of English at the University of Virginia, suggests that, in becoming teachers, we pledge to do for our students what our own best teachers did for us. Edmundson says, "Virtually all of us teachers got into the profession because we have been inspired by someone like my teacher at Medford High. We need to become determined that, as Wordsworth put it, 'what we have loved, others will love,' and we will teach them how."[8]

Research on school violence and safety by Anne Marie Lenhardt and H. Jeanette Willert suggests that students want teachers to care. They report, "The resounding message we heard from both middle and high school students was that they wanted to be listened to and taken seriously; most important they want to be respected. Connectedness, a sense of belonging and feeling cared for were top priorities for students. They seemed to believe there is a direct correlation between caring and learning."[9]

Arthur Levine,[10] former president of Teachers College, echoes a solution offered in this book, expanding the number of angel teachers, when he suggests that teachers need to have a dual qualification in both subject matter and pedagogy. It is a role in which teachers maintain their historical roles as masters of their subject areas and gain an expanded role that encourages and expects them to understand the personal side of their students' lives and how each student learns and develops.

The first step toward creating a dual role for all teachers is opening up the helping doors and inviting them into the process, even though they might have many doubts, concerns, and even fears. In my experience, the best way to get them on board is to offer them the necessary training so they begin to believe helping students with personal issues is something they can do well and include it in their teaching role.

Not every teacher will be interested, nor will they all choose the helping role after being involved in training. But effective training can encourage many teachers to take a risk, get involved, and be supported in this new role by natural allies, including angel teachers and counselors.

Using the "Teacher-as-Helper Self-Awareness Inventory"[11] is a good place to start. The inventory helps to focus teachers on what is involved, what is to come, what can go wrong, and where their support lies.

TEACHER-AS-HELPER SELF-AWARENESS INVENTORY

The purpose of this exercise is to help you assess your strengths as a helper. The following questions will help you focus on the kinds of problems and people that elicit your best helping efforts. It will also help you to identify areas that are more difficult for you and need shoring up.

- What events or influences led you to want to help others?
- Who are your models and mentors? What did they teach you about the helping process? In particular, what words and actions did they use that made them stand out as effective helpers?
- Have you modeled your professional life after some of these valued mentors? Do you use some of the same skills or words you learned from these mentors in your own helping role? Can you still hear their voices?
- Often in our own development as persons and professionals, we encounter helpers who are ineffective. While well-meaning, they lack the skills, sometimes even the interest, to be effective helpers. They often use words and actions that send a signal that *you had better look elsewhere.* Can you still hear their voices? Do you work not to become like them yourself? Please describe how these would-be helpers may have impacted your life. They missed an opportunity. Did it hurt?
- What are your personal goals in helping others? In other words, what's in it for you? What do you think you will gain from the process?

- What are your fears about the helping process? We all come into the helping process a little uneasy. Questions abound. Will there be problems you feel you can't handle? Will your uneasiness with some clients come through?
- What kinds of people and groups do you prefer to help? In spite of the wise advice in our training that we need to be inclusive, we are still human and often our response is to maintain our own level of comfort. We tend to gravitate toward certain people and groups to help, those who don't threaten our professional and personal comfort zone. Given this reality, we need to be aware of this tendency, and see it clearly, so we don't avoid "the other" who may unsettle us. We need to constantly reassess our level of inclusion and work to expand, not limit, those we embrace. For example, do you like to help women, men, the elderly, younger people, the well-educated, the economically well-off, the needy, the underdog, those left out of the mainstream, victims, etc.? Whom do you gravitate toward?
- What kinds of people and groups do you prefer not to help? We all have a dark side. We have a life experience in which we have been told to stay clear of some people and groups. The influence of our parents, peers, community, and culture may have placed limits on those whom we include and value. We are not always inclusive. For example, have you erected barriers with some clients because of age, gender, culture, color, personality, ethnicity, appearance, etc.? Whom do you avoid? Does it show?
- What kinds of problems interest you and motivate you to want to help? Again, our own background and experience often influence us to want to help with certain problems. For example, these might be problems with relationships, divorce, a gambling addiction, finances, abuse, loss and loneliness, anger and violence, etc. What is your *preferred* problem list?
- What kinds of problems do you tend to avoid, refer to others, or bluntly say "I don't do these kinds of problems"? For example, do you avoid suicide, health issues such as anorexia and bulimia, extramarital affairs, grieving, etc.? What is your "I don't want to deal with this" list?
- List your strengths as a helper. For example, are you an effective listener? Questioner? Nonjudgmental? Knowable? Able to confront when necessary? Do you know when to end the counselor-client relationship and move on? Are you able to establish a trusting and accepting relationship? Can you refer to and seek the advice of a colleague or mentor when necessary?

- At the same time, we all have areas in which we lack skills or have skills that need improvement. We can never become consummate professionals without addressing these areas. Using a baseball analogy, we are like a pitcher who, while he has a good fastball, lacks a curve and a change-up. What skills do you lack? Do you need to learn to be less judgmental? A better listener? Must you learn to engage problems you now avoid or refer? Confront when necessary? Learn when to end a helping relationship rather than holding on to it to satisfy your own personal needs for belonging and communication?
- How do you view yourself as a professional helper? Are you good at this work or just getting along?
- How do others view you as a professional helper? For example, do colleagues see you as effective? How about your clients or students? And how about family members? Do they value your helping skills?
- Effective helpers often have an informal support group with whom they can talk, receive and give feedback, and sound off about their professional and personal issues. It should come as no surprise that our professional and personal issues sometimes get meshed together. After all, when we help others we often become aware of our own personal issues that need attention. They persist and cry out for action. We are not immune to problems and we suffer the same setbacks and problems that our clients face. We are not much use to our students if we are not working at resolving our own personal issues. To keep ourselves on an even keel, we need trusted colleagues and friends who can give us honest and sometimes harsh and unpleasant feedback. List at least ten people who currently serve, or could serve, as a support group for you. These are people who make time for you and are concerned about your personal and professional development, people who know your dark side and can quickly zero in when you are heading for conflict.

This inventory can yield important data that can be used by the leaders to develop an ongoing training program based on their needs. What follows are issues, concerns, and needs for helping skills raised by over three hundred participants in a graduate level course I taught on helping and counseling students.

- The need on my part to believe I am well-trained, skilled, and have something to offer my students

- Underestimating myself and my skills
- I don't have enough knowledge and an adequate skill base about helping.
- I need to stop thinking I can save every at-risk student.
- How do I shut down, stop being weighted down by student problems and taking them home with me?
- Getting too emotionally involved with my students
- Fear of leading students down a wrong path by giving bad advice
- Inflicting my own values and opinions on vulnerable students
- Helping students with problems related to death and grieving when I am unsure about my own feelings on this issue
- As a novice helper, I am afraid my uneasiness and lack of experience will show.
- Finding peace within myself in helping others. In helping others, will I really help myself to be a better person?
- Concern that students will not relate to me and will think I am too old to understand their problems
- I might exclude students who come from different backgrounds, color, and cultures from mine.
- Wanting every students to like me even though I know this is unrealistic
- Not knowing what to do if a student offers resistance and basically tells me to get lost
- My fear of the unknown, dealing with problems and issues I have not experienced
- I am afraid students will read my uneasiness through my body language and lack of eye contact.
- I am not able to confront students—or parents or colleagues—when necessary. I have a hard time saying *no* or *that's enough*.
- Doing damage to a student because of what I say or do
- Asking the wrong questions or giving bad advice
- Talking too much
- I am nervous about leading helping groups. I prefer to help students one-on-one.
- Others think I am a better helper than I think I am. They don't realize that I am very unsure.
- Concern that students will not appreciate my efforts to help them
- I fear I don't know how to be silent and let students do the talking.
- Problems of sexual abuse and suicide make me uneasy.

- I sometimes feel the need to provide answers rather than helping students find their own solutions.
- At times I am too sensitive, a bit judgmental, and looking to give advice even when it is not asked for.
- I'm afraid of asking too many questions rather than letting the student talk.
- I don't know how to *really listen* to students.
- I'm too focused on preparing my own response rather than listening to the student.
- How can I create a quiet time so students can think quietly about their problems and possible solutions?
- I'm afraid of being judgmental even though I believe I am free of judgments.
- How can I zero in on the main problem facing a student?
- I don't know how to terminate a helping relationship and let students go their own ways, not hang onto them.
- How do I set boundaries and not get too emotionally involved with students? How can I learn not to be their parent or their friend?
- How can I develop some separation between my professional life as a helper and my personal life?
- I have to learn not to jump in too fast with a solution before the student has completed his or her story.
- I need to avoid giving too much advice and thinking I have all the answers to their problems.

Inventory responders listed problem areas that sometimes made them uneasy and in which they feel they needed more training:

- Child abuse
- Sexual abuse
- Physical abuse
- Emotional abuse
- Drug, alcohol, and tobacco addiction
- Students and teachers who are bullies
- Death and loss
- Suicide and suicidal thoughts
- Family violence
- Acting out, aggressive students
- Whining, never happy students, colleagues, and parents

- Aggressive, bullying parents

Inventory responders also listed problem areas they felt more comfortable handling:

- Failing students
- Underachieving students
- Potential dropouts
- Mentally challenged students
- Student conflict with teachers, administrators, or parents
- Family problems such as separation and divorce
- Peer problems
- Helping the underdog and isolated student
- Helping the average student who gets little attention
- Working with students who open up quickly in the helping sessions and want help
- Physically handicapped students
- Students with health issues such as obesity and eating disorders
- Students new to the school who are trying to find their way

Inventory responders listed adult role models who helped them through their own tough times as teens. Often these helpers were described as persons central to their lives, present in their daily experiences, who were willing to help them. They mentioned the following helpers:

- Classroom teacher
- Coach
- School nurse
- Minister
- Community recreation coach
- Police officer
- Neighbor
- School club director (music, theater, tutor)

The concerns, need for more training, and comfort level issues raised in this sample of potential helpers provide important data for a training team composed of angel teachers and natural allies. This data signals which issues are important to future helpers in providing them with ongoing training that can prepare them for the helping role. It's a simple but necessary intervention plan so that novice teachers can consider what is required in the helping role, develop some beginning skills, and know that additional training and support are close by. The Teacher-as-Helper Self-Awareness Inventory can be a valuable tool in assessing the needs of future teacher helpers.

Finally, the inventory serves the valuable purpose of helping novice helpers remember those adults who helped them to resolve personal problems in their own teen years. These were often adults who played a central role in their lives as teachers, coaches, or other school personnel, adults whom they saw every day and who knew them well. The inventory helps these novice helpers recall the welcoming words and behaviors of these helpers and how their overtures were successful in helping them. They are able to recall that they had helping models in their own pasts who taught them a great deal about how help is given.

The inventory also offers them the opportunity to recall those adults who seemed uncaring or remote and who were clearly not interested in offering an open door to help. As helpers ourselves, we did indeed learn much in our teen years, both from those who invited us in and from those who closed their doors to us. We know what works and what doesn't because of our own experience. Teachers have lived lives and experienced troubles along the path to adulthood. It's important to help them remember that there were important lessons learned from having troubles, having someone help them, and in the process regaining their confidence.

It is also important for novice helpers to remind themselves that helpers are human. Perhaps some of the potential helpers who failed to offer help were caring people but were overextended in their own personal and professional lives. They may have wanted to help but were trapped in a bureaucratic role and/or personal crises. Helpers can't always deliver help and that is why we need many of them available, to step in when one fails. Many open doors for help work better than just a few.

There is an important message in this limited sample of inventory responses for administrators and teachers, unions, and counselor leaders. Many teachers are interested in helping troubled students. However, they are not angel teachers who seem to arrive in the classroom with a desire and a gift for helping others. Rather, these responses tell a tale of novices who were trained as subject matter teachers in graduate school and now find themselves in a school world surrounded by students in need of personal support when they enter our large secondary schools.

Many teachers arrive in their new schools overwhelmed by the magnitude of students' personal issues and shaken by the fact that they lack the necessary skills to help these students. As education reformer John Goodlad reports, "The teacher wants to teach and the role they have in mind is a far cry from nurturing students in the personal and social non-academic aspects of their lives."[12]

This is not a problem of their making. Many teachers were not trained to be helpers in their graduate work and once in the schools were not expected to offer personal help to troubled students. The events of today have created the demand for more teachers to open their long-closed doors to students in need. As education reformers and school leaders, we can't expect them to do this helping job well unless we provide them with the necessary skills.

The responses to the inventory questions indicate the unease that teachers feel when considering a helping role. What if students reject their overtures? What if they fail to help a troubled student? Are unable to find the right words in helping? Not able to overcome resistance to helping certain students? The list goes on. There are far too few responses that indicate confidence in taking on the helping role and a belief that it's a job they can do well.

Our challenge as educators is to respond to the cries of teachers who lack the necessary skills and confidence and provide them with the tools and training they need, training that will enable them to move from being observers on the sidelines into a proactive role as helpers. We live in tough economic times where the lives of children are becoming more at-risk every day. The following are two indicators of the important need to have caring and committed teachers nearby to help them find ways out of their troubled lives.

1. Charles M. Blow[13] reports in the *New York Times* that one of the greatest casualties of the great recession may well be a decade of lost children. Blow points out that the "State of America's Children, 2011" report issued in July of 2011 by the Children's Defense Fund indicates that the impact of the recession on children's well-being has been catastrophic. Here are some of the findings:

   • The number of children living in poverty has increased by four million since 2000, and the number of children who fell into poverty between 2008 and 2009 was the largest single-year increase ever noted.

- The number of homeless children in public schools increased 41 percent between the 2006–2007 and 2008–2009 school years.
- In 2009 an average of 15.6 million children received food stamps monthly, a 65 percent increase over ten years.
- A number of children in all racial groups and 79 percent or more of black and Hispanic children in public schools cannot read or do math at grade level in the fourth, eighth, or twelfth grades.

Blow also says a report issued in August 2011 by the nonpartisan Center on Budget and Policy Priorities points out that of the forty-seven states with newly enacted budgets, thirty-eight or more states are making deep cuts in K–12 education, higher education, health care, and other key areas, even as states face rising numbers of children enrolled in public schools.

2. *New York Times* writer Alan Schwarz[14] reports that a study raises fresh questions about the effectiveness of school discipline. The study found that 31 percent of Texas students were suspended off campus or expelled at least once during their years in middle and high school, an average of almost four times apiece.

When also considering less serious infractions punished by in-school suspensions, the rate climbs to nearly 60 percent with one in seven students facing such disciplinary measures at least eleven times. The study by the Council of State Governments followed every incoming seventh grader over three years through high school.

Ross Skiba, a professor of school psychology at Indiana University, said, "The findings are very much representative of the nation as a whole." Skiba suggests that "we have enough data to show that the increase in suspensions is more than just poverty and any greater misbehavior. My guess is it's very subtle interactional effects between some teachers and students."

Schwarz also describes the reaction of Zeph Capo to the study. Capo, a former alternative education teacher in Texas, is now vice president of the Houston Federation of Teachers and trains teachers in classroom management. He appears to have a very different opinion from Skiba. Capo says:

> Sometimes there's not a lot of choice left but to risk chaos and anarchy in your school. There are potential times when human beings have had it and they drop the hammer and maybe the hammer crushes too far.

Both of these examples bring home the need to train teachers to be ready and set to help students before and when they face trouble, before they are caught up in the disciplinary system and then, for some, the legal system. Skiba suggests that one reason teens get into trouble is that there are "very subtle interactional effects between some teachers and students."

Skiba seems to be suggesting that some teachers are unprepared or unwilling to relate, instruct, like, care for, and help some students. Teachers are threatened by these students and want them out of their classes. And, as Skiba says, the reasons "are more than poverty and any greater misbehavior."

While there seems to be a huge difference between being "unprepared" and "unwilling" to help troubled students, in my experience these reasons often go hand in hand. When teachers are unprepared, unskilled, in how to instruct and intervene to help troubled teens, their response is often cloaked in a macho response such as "unwilling." That is saying, for many, "My job is to teach kids. If they don't want to be taught and behave themselves, out they go. My job is teaching, not being a social worker or counselor. If they don't want to learn, they don't belong in my class."

It appears that Capo's remarks fall into the "unwilling" category when he says that "there are potential times when human beings have had it and they drop the hammer and maybe the hammer crushes too far." Capo's use of the word "crushes" spells out exactly the devastating toll on troubled teens when they have no escape from the hammer and no advocate to intervene to hold the hammer at bay.

The word "crush" is defined as "to break or injure, bring pressure by squeezing together; crumble; pound into sand; overrule by force; oppress largely." The word "crush" is foreign to what America and American education is about. It appears often in our culture in terms of attacks on an enemy, crushing and destroying them so they are obliterated, broken.

The bottom line in this approach is that, when teachers feel they have had it, their primary source of help is to advocate for removal of the student from the classroom, not just being sent to the principal's office, after-school detention, weekend detention, or extra homework. It's a policy that gives license to and encourages the practice of removing students from the classroom on a wholesale basis, particularly teens who have no parents, other family members, or advocates to stand up for them.

This policy says to teachers, "When you feel like you are running into interference from students who are giving you trouble, our goal is a no-nonsense approach. Suspend them; expel them. That's the lesson we are trying to teach all our students—start trouble and you're done in this school. The policy of this school is to have zero tolerance for acting-out students who threaten the safety of our teachers and other students. Mischief of any kind will not be tolerated."

An analysis of data suggests that more teens are probably headed for troubled lives given the current economic climate. In these tough times many will bring their troubles to school, looking for a teacher, coach, or anyone who will listen, help them out, and stand by them. If their schools lack angel teachers and if instead the school culture, as the Texas study suggests, relies heavily on suspensions and expulsions, where can they turn before they falter and become involved in the legal system?

The study found that almost 15 percent of students, a vast majority of whom had extensive school disciplinary files, had at least one record of being in the juvenile justice system. The study found links between school discipline and criminal activity.

This is not to say that every troubled teen can be helped. No matter how much intervention is provided, some troubled teens will enter the legal system and continue to have troubled lives. But we need to train and encourage every teacher to do what they can to help teens and help the teachers themselves to find alternatives to using the hammer, risking that the hammer will crush too far and the students will crumble.

Our schools and teachers can do better. We need to show them how and loudly reject the use of the hammer as the only way to intervene.

New York Times writer Anna Phillips speaks to the growing need to have angel teachers in our schools who are willing to pay attention, take notice, and advocate for their students and make their school life safer, more welcoming, supportive, and rewarding. Phillips describes a new mobile game, "The Teachers of New York City,"[15] that turns public school teachers into heroes and heroines to improve the school life of their students. In the game a formerly upstanding New York teacher is driven crazy by constant budget cuts, school closings, and so forth and is transformed into an advocate for change.

Maybe this is only a game but it speaks to the inspiration among caring teachers to act on their own to help kids, not waiting for some distant professional to offer help that never arrives or for the green light to go ahead and offer help, counsel, and support on their own. They are trying to fill a vacuum of help created by more and more counselors being used as quasi-administrators and to regain the long-dormant role of teacher as helper and counselor as well as subject matter teacher.

Maybe the game is teaching a lesson on what can be done in real life.

NOTES

1. Joseph Sanacore, "Home at School," *Newsday*, August 2, 2002, 20 (A).
2. Deborah Meier, *In Schools We Trust* (Boston: Beacon, 2002), 10.
3. Harold Munson, "Guidance and Instruction: A Rapprochement," in *Guidance for Education in Revolution*, ed. David R. Cook, 337, 341–43 (Boston: Allyn and Bacon, 1971).
4. David R. Cook, "The Future of Guidance as a Profession," in *Guidance for Education in Revolution*, ed. David R. Cook, 517, 523–24, 529–31, 548 (Boston: Allyn and Bacon, 1971).
5. Winnie Hu, "Bullying Law Puts New Jersey Schools on Spot," *New York Times*, August 31, 2011, 1, 23 A.
6. Jacques Steinberg, "Graduates Fault Advice of Guidance Counselors," *New York Times*, March 3, 2010, A (20).
7. Jean Johnson and Jon Rochkind, "Can I Get a Little Advice?" *Public Agenda*, March 2, 2012, 12.
8. Mark Edmundson, "Soul Training," *New York Times Magazine*, August 8, 2002, 8, 10 (6).
9. Ann Marie Lenhardt and H. Jeanette Willert, "Involving Stakeholders in Resolving School Violence," *NASSP Bulletin* 86 (June 2002): 32–43.
10. Arthur Levine, "Rookies in the Schools," *New York Times*, June 29, 2002, 15 (A).
11. William L. Fibkins, "Teacher-as-Helper Self-Awareness Inventory," 2007, unpublished.
12. John J. Goodlad, *Teachers for Our Nation's Schools* (San Francisco: Jossey-Bass, 1990), 8.
13. Charles M. Blow, "The Decade of Lost Children," *New York Times*, August 6, 2011, A17.
14. Alan Schwarz, "School Discipline Study Raises Fresh Questions," *New York Times*, July 19, 2011, nytimes.com/2011/07/19/education/19/dicsipline.html_r1&pagewanted=pr, accessed August 1, 2011.
15. Anna A. Phillips, "Shuttered Schools? In Game, Heroic Teachers Save the Day," *New York Times*, October 26, 2011, 25 (A).

References

Agee, James. *A Death in the Family*. New York: Bantam, 1957.
Belcher, David. "Sheen's Circle, From Son to Father." *New York Times*, February 23, 2010.
Berkow, Ira. "An Athlete Is Dead at 17 and No One Can Say Why." *New York Times*, October 1, 1995.
Bill and Melinda Gates Foundation. National Education Summit on High Schools, blogoehlert.typepad.com/eclippings/2005/05/bill_gates_amer.html (accessed October 25, 2011).
Blow, Charles. "The Decade of Lost Children." *New York Times*, August 6, 2011.
Cook, David R. "The Future of Guidance as a Profession." *Guidance for Education in Revolution*, ed. David R. Cook. Boston: Allyn and Bacon, 1971.
Edmundson, Mark. "Soul Training." *New York Times Magazine*, August 8, 2002.
Fibkins, William L. *Innocence Denied: A Guide to Preventing Sexual Misconduct by Teachers and Coaches*. Lanham, MD: Rowman & Littlefield, 2006.
———. *Teen Obesity: How Schools Can Be the Number One Solution to the Problem*. Lanham, MD: Rowman & Littlefield, 2006.
———. *An Administrator's Guide to Better Teacher Mentoring*. Lanham, MD: Rowman & Littlefield, 2011.
———. "Teacher-as-Helper Self-Awareness Inventory." 2007 (unpublished).
Goodlad, John J. *Teachers for Our Nation's Schools*. San Francisco: Jossey-Bass, 1990.
Hampton, Wilborn. "Horton Foote, Chronicler of America in Plays and Films." *New York Times*, March 5, 2009.
Hendrie, Caroline. "Abuse by Women Raises Its Own Set of Problems." *Education Week*, December 2, 1998. www.edweek.org/ew/vol-18/14women.h.18 (accessed August 13, 2004).
Hu, Winnie. "Bullying Law Puts New Jersey Schools on Spot." *New York Times*, August 31, 2011.
Johnson, Jean, and Jon Rochkind. "Can I Get a Little Advice?" *Public Agenda*, March 2010.
Keller, Bill. "I Yield My Time to the Gentleman from Stratford-Upon-Avon." *New York Times Magazine*, August 14, 2011.
Lenhardt, Ann Marie, and H. Jeanette Willert. "Involving Stakeholders in Resolving School Violence." *NASSP Bulletin*, June 2002.

Levine, Arthur. "Rookies in the Schools." *New York Times*, June 29, 2002.

Longman, Jere. "An Athlete's Dangerous Experiment." *New York Times*, November 26, 2003.

Meier, Deborah. *In Schools We Trust*. Boston: Beacon, 2002.

Munson, Harold. "Guidance and Instruction: A Rapprochement." *Guidance for Education in Revolution*, ed. David R. Cook. Boston: Allyn & Bacon, 1971.

Phillipson, Anna A. "Shuttered Schools? In Game, Heroic Teachers Save the Day." *New York Times*, October 26, 2011.

Sanacore, Joseph. "Home at School." *Newsday*, August 2, 2002.

Santora, Marc. "Case Tries to Link a Mother to Her Boy's Suicide." *New York Times*, September 27, 2003.

Schwarz, Alan. "School Discipline Study Raises Fresh Questions." *New York Times*, July 19, 2011. www.nytimes.com/2011/07/19/education/19/discipline.html_r1&pagewanted=pr (accessed August 1, 2011).

Smith, Estelle Lander. "Teen to Testify at Teacher Sex Trial." *Newsday*, May 6, 1994.

Steinberg, Jacques. "Graduates Fault Advice of Guidance Counselors." *New York Times*, March 3, 2010.

Yan, Eileen, and Robin Topping. "School Sex Abuse: Sachem H.S. Teacher Held in Case Involving Teen." *Newsday*, June 25, 1993.

About the Author

William L. Fibkins is an author and educational consultant specializing in training programs for school administrators, teachers, pupil service professionals, support staff, students, and parents. He holds degrees in school administration, counselor education, and health education from Syracuse University and the University of Massachusetts.

www.ingramcontent.com/pod-product-compliance
Lightning Source LLC
Chambersburg PA
CBHW051815230426
43672CB00012B/2743